SIGNS OF CERTAINTY

THE LINGUISTIC IMPERATIVE IN FRENCH CLASSICAL LITERATURE

STANFORD FRENCH AND ITALIAN STUDIES

volume LXXI

DEPARTMENT OF FRENCH AND ITALIAN
STANFORD UNIVERSITY

SIGNS OF CERTAINTY

THE LINGUISTIC IMPERATIVE IN FRENCH CLASSICAL LITERATURE

BARBARA R. WOSHINSKY

1991

ANMA LIBRI

Stanford French and Italian Studies is a collection of scholarly publications devoted to the study of French and Italian literature and language, culture and civilization. Occasionally it will allow itself excursions into related Romance areas.

Stanford French and Italian Studies will publish books, monographs, and collections of articles centering around a common theme, and is open to scholars associated with academic institutions other than Stanford.

The collection is published by the Department of French and Italian, Stanford University and ANMA Libri.

LC 90-86348
ISBN 0-915838-87-7

Printed in the United States of America.

Contents

To David,
involuntary francophile

Acknowledgements

This book owes its existence to many individuals and organizations. I would like to acknowledge the National Endowment for the Humanities, which gave my research its original impetus; the Bunting Institute of Radcliffe College, for its stimulating and sustaining atmosphere; the Max Orovitz Fund of the University of Miami, for its generous and repeated support; the Camargo Foundation in Cassis, where I spent a fruitful fall completing my revisions and finally, the most timely assistance of the Michel de Certeau Center for Critical Studies. Many thanks to Maria Reynardus, the one-woman Word Processing Service of the College of Arts and Sciences, University of Miami, for her patient collaboration. Above all, I am grateful to the friends and colleagues who have unstintingly offered their encouragement and inspiration throughout the years. Most special thanks to Jules Brody, Erica Harth, Christine Raffini, Sylvie Romanowski, Harvey Siegel, David Rubin, Michael Schub, Bill Turner, and Charles Williams; and, of course, to my parents.

Coral Gables, Florida, June 1990

Permissions

Portions of previously published articles by Barbara Woshinsky appear in this volume in modified form:

"Rhetorical Vision in *Le Cid*," *French Forum* 4.2 (May 1979) 147-59.

"Biblical Discourse: Reading the Unreadable," *L'Esprit Créateur* 21.1 (Summer 1981) 13-24.

"*Britannicus*: Truth and Its Image," *Analecta Husserliana* 17.4 (November 1981) 417-23. A. T. Tymieniecka, ed. Reprinted by permission of Kluwer Academic Publishers. Dordrecht, Boston, Lancaster: D. Reidel Publishing.

"Pascal's *Pensées* and the Discourse of the Inexpressible," *Papers on French Seventeenth Century Literature* 7.14 (1980-1981) 57-65; "Shattered Speech: La Bruyère, de la cour 81," *PFSCL* 8.15, 2 (1981) 211-26; "'Aimer un bras': Metonymic Mutilation in Corneille's *Horace*," *PFSCL* 12.22 (1985) 237-46; "Image, Representation, Idea," *PFSCL* 25 (1986) 227-42; "*Esther*: No Continuing Place," in Richard L. Barnett, ed. *Relectures raciniennes*, Etudes Littéraires Françaises (Tübingen: G. Narr, 1986) 227-42.

"La Bruyère's *Caractères*: A Typographical Reading," *TEXT* 2 (1985) 209-28 (© 1985 by AMS Press, Inc.).

"Classical Uncertainties," *Continuum* (1988) 133-49 (© 1989 by AMS Press, Inc.).

1. Introduction

> Language, then, is no longer to be a calumny, no longer a falsifier of what it relates; it is to be a bearer of truth.
>
> Timothy Reiss, *Tragedy and Truth* 259

> As I was going up the stair
> I met a man who wasn't there
> He wasn't there again today
> I wish, I wish he'd stay away.
>
> Hughes Mearnes, *The Psychoed* 938

This study examines the epistemological status of classical literature: the relations between literary language and truth in the seventeenth century. In order to limit this vast topic, I have focused on a close analysis of representative texts. To explore the boundaries of classical discourse, I have chosen two dramatists (Corneille, Racine), an essayist (La Bruyère), and a theologian (Pascal). This choice brings to the fore similarities and contrasts in genre and linguistic function. For example, both Corneille and Racine call Aristotelian concepts of dramatic representation into question, but in very different ways. Similarly, Pascal and La Bruyère produce fragmented, discontinuous forms, but their use of fragmentation differs both stylistically and epistemologically. One of the goals of this study is to examine these differences and their implications.

At the same time, this topic raises fundamental issues which transcend period, genre and author. First of all, what is "literary language"? What, for that matter, is truth, and how is one to be found in the other? Finally, what confusions, or fertile interrelations, exist between classical and modern epistemologies? Although I am addressing these issues in my introduction, any satisfactory answers must come from the body of the text and the quality of its readings. For all works comment on their own process, both explicitly and implicitly, and it is the task of the interpreter to elucidate these comments. Thus, good reading will always precede and supersede good theory. However, the propositions are not reversible: theory, whatever its importance, does not always make good reading, especially for nonspecialists. By using a concrete textual approach, I hope to provide useful and accessible insights for undergraduate literary studies as well as matter for more abstract speculations.

Does literary language have a special identity which distinguishes it from other statements humans make about the world? Many writers would say so. Michael Riffaterre, for example, emphasizes the uniqueness of poetic discourse: "the language of poetry differs from common linguistic usage — this much the most unsophisticated reader senses instinctively." What does the difference consist of? "To put it very simply, a poem says one thing and means another" (1). This shift from "saying" to "meaning" is accomplished by the presence of anomalous terms, which create heretofore-unsuspected connections — "abysses," in Riffaterre's parlance. The reader, caught in these abysses, can only find her way out by building new semantic bridges — in other words, by reinterpreting the text. Reading thus becomes an act of reorientation which moves the text away from representation: "Let's give up the criterion that meanings must conform to reality and replace it with the criterion of conformity with words" (33). And verisimilitude amounts to a readerly state of mind, not an actual relation between text and "reality."

In *Blindness and Insight*, Paul de Man also speaks of "the distinctive characteristics of literary language." He attacks the "demystifying critics" who deny the privileged nature of literature: "For the statement about language, that sign and meaning can never coincide, is what is precisely taken for granted in the kind of language we call literary. Literature, unlike everyday language, begins on the far side of this knowledge; it is the only form of language free from the fallacy of immediate expression... fiction is not myth, for it knows and names itself as fiction" (17-18). In contrast, another trend in Continental criticism, finding its roots in linguistics and philosophy, refuses any special status to literary discourse. According to Steven Lynn, "scientists and literary critics should adopt the same attitude toward the epistemological status of their respective discourses" (1). It is as though for Lynn, all discourse is truth, whereas for de Man, all discourse is fiction — except only fiction knows it, thereby declaring its difference.

The examination of literary discourse has quickly led us to the question of literary truth, for "the relationship among descriptive 'representation,' fiction and reality," is a complex and interdependent one. But when we try to distill a specific "truth" from literature, the difficulties become even greater. For the truth of literature, like the little man in Mearnes' poem,[1] is tantalizingly present in its absence. As educated readers, we know that fiction is not true to life in a literal sense: unlike the lady in the evening course on literary masterpieces, we will not say of Flaubert's heroine, "She never should've married that Bovary character in the first place." However, this anecdote does not imply any sense of superiority. Our own position is equally vulnerable: whatever "method" we follow, whatever its degree of sophistication, reading involves a search for meaning, which ultimately becomes a search for truth.

Jacques Derrida has recently shown both the futility of this search and its inevitability.[2] For Derrida, the "little man who wasn't there" is the illusion of meaning, truth, or ultimate being, that we still vainly seek to discover within, above, or beyond words. Meaning is never really there because words constantly refer (or, in Derrida's language, *de*fer) to one another, in an endless succession. A roughly analogous experience we have probably all had is looking up a word in a dictionary (preferably a foreign dictionary, for a language we do not know very well). The word is always defined in terms of other words which, if one continues to follow the references, eventually lead back to the unintelligible word we looked up in the first place. Meaning, as James Thurber says, is "otherwhere than here, otherwhen than now" (*White Deer* 15). I am reminded of the scene in Thurber's *White Deer* where a group of smiling characters are holding tragic masks. Chuckling and chortling to themselves, they chorus: "We wear our masks on yesterdays and on tomorrows... And since those sad days never come — ... We know no sorrows" (54). Perhaps we could think of Derrida's meanings as *deferred* in this way. Often, it is in works of so-called "nonsense," which stretch language to the breaking point, that certain philosophical issues can be seen most clearly.

[1] Quoted in *Familiar Quotations*, ed. John Bartlett, 14th edition (Boston: Little, Brown, 1968) 938.

[2] Cf. *L'Ecriture et la différence* (Paris: 1967); *De la grammatologie* (Paris: Minuit, 1967), English translation by Gayatyri C. Spivak (Baltimore: Johns Hopkins University Press, 1976).

The paradox of meaning has another side. By making a statement like "there are no definitive statements," we plunge back into a truth-centered view of language, because for this statement to be intelligible we must have an idea of what a definitive statement would be — or at least think we have. Wrong implies right, and false implies true; we cannot escape these antitheses because we literally think through them. Under such circumstances, perhaps all that is left to do is to grasp both ends of the paradox and hold on. In other words, instead of looking for *the* truth behind the words on the page, we move back one step and examine the concept of truth as it is set forth in the writings of a given period or author. This is what I propose to do, or to begin doing, with seventeenth-century French literature, because the truth-centered view of language was explicitly defined in that century. And to some degree, as we will see, modern linguistic thought still bears the French classical stamp.

How did classical theorists conceive of the relation between words and truth? Throughout most of Western history, philosophers have regarded language as an expression of mental process. The role of discourse, for I. A. Richards as for Plato, is to transform itself into the transparent envelope of the thought it bears. The utopic end point of this process, according to the seventeenth-century French philosopher Malebranche, is to communicate not with mere words, but by pure ideas alone. And it was in the seventeenth century that the close connection between language and thought, and the identification of thought with truth, became the foundation for linguistic theory. As Hobbes wrote in the *Leviathan*, "The general use of speech is to transfer our mental discourse into verbal; or the train of our thoughts into a train of words."[3] Speech is linear because thought is linear. The French logicians and grammarians of Port-Royal shared this view. The first sentence of the Port-Royal *Grammar*, published in 1660, reads: "To speak is to explain one's thoughts by signs, which men invented to that purpose." ("Parlez, est expliquer ses pensees par des signes, que les hommes ont inventez a ce dessin."[4]) Hence Port-Royal theory takes Locke one step further: not only does language serve to express thought, but it was deliberately invented for that purpose. This teleology of expressiveness permeates the Port-Royal *Grammar* down to the smallest details. Take the explanation of pronouns: since people often had to talk about the same things and it would have been

[3] Ch. 4, "Of Speech" (Oxford: Clarendon, 1967) 24.

[4] Reprint of 1660 edition (Menston, England: Scolar Press, 1967) 5, my translation.

rude for them to repeat themselves, they invented words to take the place of nouns. For this reason they called them pronouns (56). Similarly, the personal pronoun *I* (*je*) was invented out of modesty (a reluctance to speak about oneself). This fusion of grammar with civility is more than a curtsy to the age of Louis XIV, because politeness itself serves the basic end of communication — the clear expression of thought. The speaker uses the pronoun *I*, instead of his whole name, to avoid standing in his own light — a light that he wishes to fall first and foremost on the ideas his discourse expresses.

Although the rationalism of the Port-Royal *Grammar* may appear a little quaint and outdated, its basic assumptions about communication have not been superseded in modern linguistic theory. Thus, in Pierre Giraud's *Semiology*, published in 1971, we read: "The function of the sign is to communicate ideas by means of messages" (5). If we compare this to the Port-Royal statement, "To speak is to explain one's thoughts by signs," the classical connection becomes clear. Beneath its modern linguistic apparatus, semiotics continues to regard language as a medium for communicating intellectual content. Yet at the same time, modern linguistics and its offshoots have thrown a new light on the relations between language and thought, history and literature. I am referring to the concept of discourse, in the broad sense of the communicative and symbolic systems which underpin social acts. Instead of examining what people think, the student of discourse tries to understand how, at a given period, thought was possible, to elucidate the unconscious preconditions for knowledge which are linked to, and discernible through, language. As Karlis Racerskis puts it in his book on Michel Foucault, "Instead of seeking to circumscribe meaningful discourses with the familiar devices of commentary or interpretation, Foucault wishes to reveal the historical conditions that make a particular mode of conceptualization possible" (16).

This central role afforded to language has important implications for literature. As a verbal medium, it exists on the same plane of reference as other representative systems and can be compared to these systems across the board. According to LaCapra, "nothing is seen as being purely and simply inside or outside texts. Indeed the problem becomes one of rethinking the concepts of 'inside' and 'outside' in relation to processes of interaction between language and the world... to see how the notion of textuality makes explicit the question of the relationships among uses of language, other signifying practices and various models of human activity that are bound up with processes of signification" (26-27). This notion is important to criticism because it radically alters the traditional relation between literature and ideas. If the unconscious preconditions of thought are present in language in general, they should also be present, and discernible, in literary language in particular. Thus, philosophy is not something which must be "related" to literature; to paraphrase LaCapra, it is "in" literature already. And intellectual history is no longer a matter of opinion or influences, but of words.

The linguistic model has also fostered a new approach to periodization which has changed our picture of the seventeenth century. A number of philosophers, linguists and critics now consider the classical period as a threshold between linguistic views. According to this theory, before the late sixteenth century, the world was perceived as a chain of resemblances reaching from the Creator down to the humblest of His creation. At that point, a major change is presumed to have taken place in the epistemological outlook. Through a process of secularization whose causes are unexplained — or inexplicable — God was brusquely separated from the world. The divine order still existed on high, but for practical purposes it was removed from human ken. The old hierarchical order was shattered, leaving in its place not yet the radical relativism of modern times, but an array of discrete moral/verbal principles — shards of belief. Vision is no longer whole, not yet wholly subjective: it is prismatic. This is the age of the "perspective mind."[5]

According to Sylvie Romanowski, the resulting qualitative gap between medieval and modern thought cannot be overemphasized: "Aucune commune mesure entre les deux mondes scolastique et galiléen: la destruction des ressemblances illusoires a fait place à un monde divisé entre perception et réalité. Ainsi la vérité se trouve dans la différence, qui, rappelons-le, est un trait opposé à la ressemblance, l'une des deux composantes de l'illusion" (26). The effects of this division can be felt across the spectrum of discourse, from art to philosophy to science to metaphysics. But the religious and scientific crisis of the classical age is also, and above all, a crisis of the word. Before the classical age, language partook of a cosmic analogy: as Michel Foucault puts it, words and things resembled one another. Since that time, language has no longer been considered part of the created universe; it simply represents that universe, like a grid of street names laid over

[5] See Timothy Reiss' introduction to *Yale French Studies* 49 (1973), *Science, Language and the Perspective Mind.*

a map. This shift from revelation to representation changes, but does not destroy, the power of language. In fact, the notion of representation, which runs through all classical discourses, affords us a new entry into their interrelations, similarities and differences. These interrelations, and the central position occupied by representation, are illustrated in figure 1.

Art	Mimesis [vraisemblance]	Illusion
Science/Philosophy	Representation	Error
Metaphysics	Truth	Falsehood
Religion	Perfection [divine]	Flaw [human]

Figure 1

As the diagram in figure 1 implies, classical epistemology is reality- or truth-centered, and it is the aim of discourse to convey this reality. The central column of figure 1, with its changes in terminology, expresses the various means by which reality can be represented through discourse. The right-hand column indicates the failure of accurate representation. These categories, far from being exclusive, display much overlap and ambiguity. For example, "illusion" can be considered either as flawed mimesis (as in *invraisemblance*) or as a necessary concomitant to mimesis (as in *illusion dramatique*). This relation, however, is not reciprocal: a work of art, which imitates reality rather than making true claims about it, cannot logically be accused of "error." In the central column, there is also continuity between metaphysical truth and divine perfection, but representation, in its primary sense, must cease at the divine (transcendent) level. In a secondary sense, discourse can be said to represent (*figurer*) God, as in biblical texts.

It is the term "representation" itself, however, that is the most ambivalent and all-encompassing. It cuts across several categories since it can signify either artistic portrayal (in the sense of *figurer*) or philosophical conceptualization (in the sense of *représenter à l'esprit*). These complex interconnections require a diagram to themselves (figure 2). Representation, in its dual sense of mental concept and esthetic portrayal, thus finds itself at the intersection of art and philosophy.

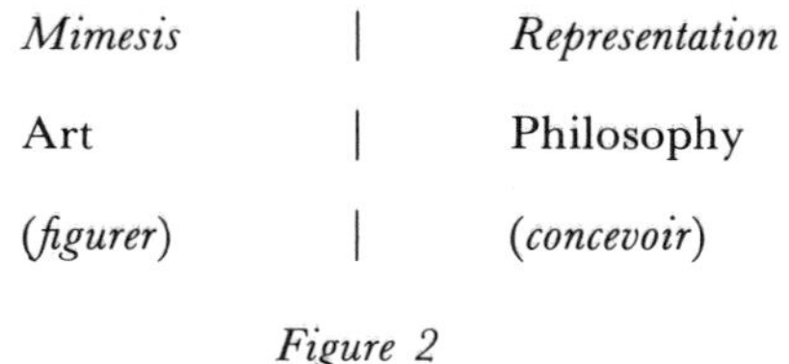

Figure 2

The theories of Foucault and his followers have, not surprisingly, given rise to much philosophical controversy. For example, in an article in the *London Review of Books*, David Hoy calls Foucault's early work relativist and structuralist, terms which, in his usage, appear equally and synonymously damning: "Where Foucault's thinking becomes particularly difficult to understand is not so much in his social criticism as in his conceptions of knowledge and truth. During his earlier, structuralist phase he seemed to be relativizing knowledge to whatever discourse happened to be spoken at a particular time, and to be denying the possibility of serious truth" (18). Foucault's work indeed posits an underlying system of assumptions that constitute the conditions of meaning: in Daniel Stempel's formulation, "the given becomes significant only through its participation in the *order* of representation" (389). In that sense, perhaps, Foucault may be called a "structuralist." However, his theory seems to me to be less relativist than *relational*: in Foucault's own words, he seeks to define "the total set of *relations* that unite, at a given period, the discursive practices that give rise to epistemological figures, sciences and possibly formalized systems" (*Archaeology of Knowledge* 191). Since knowledge changes, ideas change, through time, Hoy's notion of "serious" truth as a kind of ahistorical absolute appears difficult to defend.

The question of intellectual change is related to another controversial point in Foucault's theory. Instead of viewing thought in terms of continuity and evolution, he speaks of upheaval and rupture. Like Thomas Kuhn and Charles Taylor, Foucault asserts that ideas can take sudden, qualitative leaps: "the conceptual mutations in human history can and frequently do produce conceptual webs which are incommensurable, that is, where the terms can't be defined in relation to a common stratum of expressions" (Taylor 49). In *The Movement of Thought*, Herbert De Ley attempts to reconcile the two apparently antithetical intellectual models of rupture and evolution by applying "various sorts of empirical tinkering" to Foucault's concepts (De Ley 150). De Ley's attempts at reconciliation are not wholly successful, perhaps because theoretical concepts do not respond well to "tinkering." For my part, I find the discomfort caused by the notion of discontinuity neither surprising nor disturbing. Rethinking our intellectual history with the mental apparatus inherited from our own culture is a bold and experimental enterprise, inevitably involving concepts which are neither totally clear nor under control. In such circumstances, feeling uncomfortable is, colloquially speaking, part of the deal. Further, Foucault seems to offer his concept of sudden epistemic shifts not as a definitive solution, but as an acknowledgement of the poverty of previous solutions. What Paul de Man calls the "genetic" concept of history — "a temporal hierarchy that resembles a parental structure in which the past is like an ancestor" (*Blindness and Insight* 164) — is now recognized as part of our intellectual inheritance from nineteenth-century science. It is difficult to see how nineteenth-century notions of "history" and "evolution" can help us, in the twentieth century, to elucidate seventeenth-century thought. If anachronistic we must be, at least let us keep our anachronisms up-to-date.

What is more troubling than the notion of discontinuity is the corollary, less present in Foucault than in his followers, that an abrupt change in mind set gave rise, in the early seventeenth century, to a coherent, "dominant" world view based on accurate representation. Timothy Reiss, in *The Discourse of Modernism*, makes a forceful argument for this view.[6] In my own work on the classical period, however, I have found that "new" linguistic views do not totally abolish the old, and in fact the most illuminating insights can come from the interplay of both.[7] For all its trappings of modernity, Reiss' holistic image of the classical period bears an ironic resemblance to the "Age of Reason" long propounded by the literary orthodoxy. In my view, neither the traditional nor the "modernist" interpretation really addresses the unsettling questions posed by contemporary criticism and philosophy: questions about how social history works, how language works and how minds work. All these questions are provocatively raised by Richard Rorty.

Rorty's contribution to seventeenth-century studies, notably in *The Mirror of Nature*, is both considerable and double-edged. On the one hand, his repeated, and emphatic, tributes to classical thinkers would warm any *dix-septiémiste*'s heart: "We owe the notion of a 'theory of

[6] Cf. La Capra's extremely interesting criticism of Reiss (*Rethinking* 69-71n24).
[7] See my article on *Don Juan*, 408.

knowledge' based on an understanding of 'mental processes' to the seventeenth century, and especially to Locke. We owe the notion of 'the mind' as a separate entity in which 'processes' occur to the same period, and especially to Descartes" (3-4). Rorty concurs with Foucault and Reiss that representation has been the dominant model of thought since the seventeenth century: "To know is to represent accurately what is outside the mind... Philosophy's central concern is to be a general theory of representation" (Rorty 3). However, seventeenth-century chauvinism quickly fades when we realize that Rorty is building up classical representation only in order to demolish it: "... the notion of knowledge as accurate representation, made possible by special mental processes, and intelligible through a general theory of representation, needs to be abandoned" (6).

Clearly, Rorty's attack on classical representation is not, or is only secondarily, historical. His real target is contemporary philosophy. He points out that the notion of philosophy as a discipline centering on epistemology as a foundation for the sciences and, in fact, the notion that the sciences *need* such an epistemic foundation, are creations of the seventeenth century. But Rorty expounds this view in order to argue that it is 300 years out of date: "since the period of Descartes and Hobbes, the assumption that scientific discourse was normal discourse and that all other discourse needed to be modeled upon it has been the standard motive for philosophizing" (387). Leaving the philosophers to defend themselves against this accusation, which they are certainly well equipped to do, I will concentrate on the analogous dilemma posed to literary theory. It would be ironic if theorists, seeking a more solidly "scientific" basis for their work than nineteenth-century Kantian esthetics, were to find they had accepted a concept of science which is doubly anachronistic.[8] However, in a fittingly Cartesian way, this undermining of previous certainties may yet supply a point of departure for the reorganization of literary knowledge. To clarify this point, I need to examine the current state of interdisciplinary relations.

It is both paradoxical and revealing that Richard Rorty's argument draws its ammunition not from philosophy, but from recent work in literary theory. Nor is he alone in this: the current *rapprochement* between critical methods and those of other disciplines is fueling both research and controversy. Consider the following quotation: "When reading the works of an important thinker, look first for the apparent

[8] This argument is made by André Lefever in *Literary Knowledge*.

absurdities in the text and ask yourself how a sensible person could have written them. When you find an answer, when these passages make sense, then you may find that more central passages, ones you previously thought you understood, have changed their meaning." We may think we are reading a post-modern critic, but the author of this passage is the philosopher of science Thomas Kuhn (*The Essential Tension* xii). Similarly, "[Hayden] White looks to literary criticism for interpretative methods that may illuminate problems in historiography" (LaCapra 73). And in anthropology, Clifford Geertz has recently posed some of the same issues:

> Whether or not 'natural history' is a crime in the mind, it no longer seems quite so natural, either to those who read it or to those who write it... Once ethnographic texts begin to be looked *at* as well as through, once they are seen to be made, and made to persuade, those who make them have rather more to answer for. (137-38)

Conversely, literary critics are attracted to philosophers like Derrida not, as John Searle suggests, out of a naive "logical positivism" (78) but out of a recognition of common problems and methods. According to Searle himself, two of Derrida's main deconstructive strategies — "to look for certain key words in the text that, so to speak, give the game away," and "to pay close attention to marginal features of the text such as the sort of metaphors that occur in it" (77) — are basic techniques of textual analysis. In explaining why philosophers should disdain Derrida, Searle unwittingly reveals why some critics are stimulated by him. What is marginal to Searle is central to us.

No wonder, then, that Rorty incurs such wrath among analytic philosophers. Not only does he suggest that philosophy is closer to literature than to science, but, to add insult to injury, he founds his argument on literary techniques. He claims that the whole basis of Western rationalism — the human mind contemplating, or reflecting, truth, and thereby creating a foundation for knowledge — rests on a misplaced "ocular metaphor": the eye in the mirror.[9] The eye Rorty refers to is the Greek "eye of the mind," the mirror, Shakespeare's "Glassy Essence," both of which are given a renewed and authoritative form in the late seventeenth century. Rorty claims, with playful

[9] This view can be compared to Louis Marin's that mind is the mirror of things, language the mirror of the mind: discourse is not representation, but re-representation ("Puss in Boots," *Diacritics* 7).

skepticism, that there is no particular reason *why* this ocular metaphor seized the imagination of the founders of Western thought:

> The notion of 'contemplation,' of knowledge of universal concepts or truths as *theoria*, makes the Eye of the Mind an inescapable model for the better sort of knowledge. But it is fruitless to ask whether the Greek language, or Greek economic conditions, or the idle fancy of some nameless pre-Socratic, is responsible for viewing this sort of knowledge as *looking* at something (rather than, say, rubbing up against it, or crushing it underfoot, or having sexual intercourse with it). (38-39)

As Rorty would have it, the long search for philosophical certainty is the result of an arbitrary, almost accidental turning, not of thought, but of phrase — a rogue metaphor that should henceforth be purged from our intellectual vocabulary.

Rorty's refreshingly irreverent analysis is full of fascinating contradictions. On the one hand, by implying that representation is not "seriously" philosophical because it is not an idea but a metaphor, he appears to rejoin philosophers like Paul Ricoeur who show a Platonic suspicion of the figurative. In *The Rule of Metaphor*, "Ricoeur is himself concerned with the excessive encroachment of the poetic on the philosophic..." (LaCapra 143). But at the same time, Rorty's intellectual sympathies clearly lie with those thinkers who, like Thomas Kuhn, challenge the distinctions made by analytic philosophy:

> To sum up the line I am taking about Kuhn and his critics: the controversy between them is about whether science, as the discovery of what is really out there in the world, differs in its patterns of argumentation from discourses for which the notion of 'correspondence to reality' seems less apposite (i.e. politics and literary criticism). (332)

Rorty thus seems to be sitting on the disciplinary fence: he willingly adopts methods from literary analysis, but uses them in order to discredit philosophy for being too "literary" and imagistic.

The dominance of imagery in literature, however, is of no embarrassment to a literary critic. In fact, it may supply the link we were seeking, the central nexus or point of intersection between philosophy and literature on the one hand and representation and mimesis on the other. It is now possible to add a new dimension to the diagram sketched in figure 2, as in the "close-up" look in figure 3. The centrality of the image in esthetic representation stands on traditional ground and requires no justification; but, as the preceding discussion has implied, imagery also plays an important role in the conscious or unconscious processes of philosophic thought. Philosophers, like poets, are entrapped and enriched by the carnality of words.

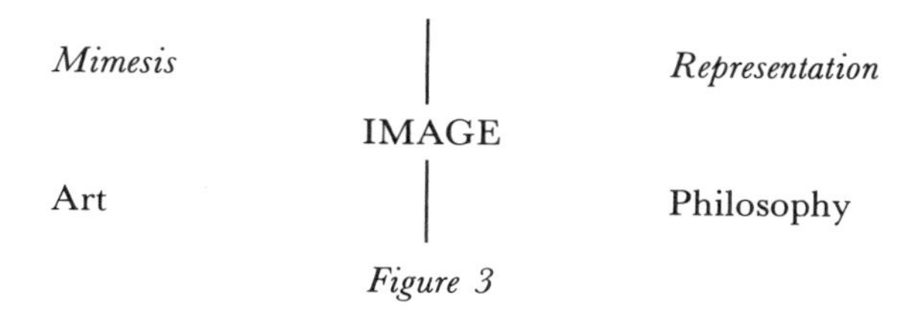

Figure 3

What connections can be drawn between this analysis and the philosophical issues raised earlier? As LaCapra asks, "What is the relationship between metaphor and model or between model and mathematics" (108) or, for that matter, between philosophy and criticism or text and thought? As a limited answer to these questions, I would suggest that the relation is partly in the eye of the beholder. It is a truism that one finds, to some extent, what one is looking for. Literary analysis may reveal different things about texts than philosophical analysis because the literary analyst seeks to elucidate meanings rather than to test claims. Critics are more comfortable with — even enjoy — contradictory, coexisting meanings, and they have elaborated techniques to unearth and deal with them. Etymology and contextual reading, for example, can help unravel the varied senses in which the world is represented; and in the unravelling process, the relations between these senses come a little more clearly into view.

While, as we have seen, Rorty also uses the concept of figurative language, his method and aims are quite different. He holds up his metaphorical mirror to prove a point, and picks his examples accordingly: a practice certainly not limited to philosophers.[10] But in jumping from the Greeks to the seventeenth century, Rorty fails to see, or at least to mention, the other glass that flashes its occult light through Western thought — *per speculum in aenigmate*, the clouded mirror of

[10] Thus, Serge Doubrovsky says of Corneille's style: "... Le jeu de mots n'est nullement antithèse gratuite; il est fin en soi, dans la mesure où il crée un univers dans lequel les problèmes humains se donnent comme *alternative indépassable* et *choix ... absolu*" (*Dialectique du heros* 37). Accordingly, in Doubrovsky's interpretation of Corneille, it is not surprising that elements of language take on the philosophical or psychological significance he attributes to the work as a whole.

Scriptural epistemology. In her study of medieval thought, *The Mirror of Language*, Rosamund Colish points out that the "dark glass" of lst Corinthians is not a *visual* image but a *verbal* one: in the original Greek, *aenigma* means "allusive or obscure speech." Like the Sphinx's riddle, it is a rhetorical device involving the use of subtle and puzzling discourse. Augustine, himself trained as a rhetorician, defines the *aenigma* as "a kind of simile but obscure and hard to understand" (*de Trinitate* XV.ix.15-16). For Augustine any theological statement is an *aenigma* because God is both unspeakable and spoken of.

This figure passed from Augustine into medieval philosophy, becoming a kind of model for theological knowledge. According to St. Anselm, "We know and express God... *through words*, as through a reflection in a mirror" (Colish 137). Anselm's own language on this point is itself "enigmatic" in the rhetorical sense: "And in this way, we often express and yet do not express, see and yet do not see, one and the same object, we express it and see it through another; we do not express it, and do not see it by virtue of its own proper nature" (quoted in Colish 138). This view of language, assimilated by Scholasticism, became part of Descartes' philosophical heritage. It might be the task of another scholar, trained in medieval philosophy, to find to what extent, and in what form, these ideas persist in modern thought. The least one can say, however, is that in place of one mirror, we have two: Rorty's intellectual glass, doubling reflection with double clarity, and Augustine's rhetorical one, connoting not just obscurity, as is commonly thought, but *indirection*; knowledge conveyed through the distorting mirror of language.

In these examples — Rorty's and Colish's — the use of methods associated with literary, rather than philosophical, analysis, gives rise to an "archeology of knowledge" different from Foucault's. For the critic, language cannot be split into geological layers; its meanings continue to persist, to a greater or lesser degree, throughout time. Semantics is an aggregate of which the writer is only partly in command: above and beyond her individual choices, conscious and unconscious, language continues to mean through, and to enrich, her text. And fiction both reveals assumptions about truth and creates them through the power of language. That is why critics looking for ways in which truths are held may find more than they are looking for — if they keep their eyes open.

2. Rhetorical Vision in Corneille

A theory of rhetorical style will always invoke a theory of motive, a theory of identity, and a theory of knowledge.
Richard Lanham, *The Motives of Eloquence* 210

We are living in an age of images. Discussions of language, intention and style dominate not only literary journals, but also news broadcasting and the Sunday supplements. Perhaps for this reason, formal rhetoric is now undergoing a surprising revival[1]: surprising because, throughout the ages, rhetoric has received a generally bad press. Thus, in 1733, Oliver Goldsmith, in his *Essay on the Theatre*, described tragic rhetoric as "the pompous train, the swelling phrase, and the unnatural rant" (III.209). Yet in recent years, as Richard Lanham observes, "by whatever aperiodic ambages, the passion for rhetoric seems to have returned" (223). And, according to Roland Barthes, "le monde est incroyablement plein d'ancienne rhétorique" (172).

The rediscovery of rhetoric has also been extended to Corneille. Whereas the major studies of past decades emphasized the moral and psychological dimensions of Corneille's work,[2] critics are now examin-

[1] Cf. Chaim Perelman and L. Olbrechts-Tyteca, *La Nouvelle Rhétorique* (Paris: PUF, 1958); Peter France, *Racine's Rhetoric* (Oxford: Clarendon, 1965); Peter Dixon, *Rhetoric* (London: Methuen, 1971); and *The Influence of Rhetoric on Seventeenth-Century French Literature*, special issue of *Papers on French Seventeenth-Century Literature* 3 (1975).

[2] Cf., for example, Paul Bénichou, *Morales du grand siècle* (Paris: Gallimard, 1948); Serge Doubrovsky, *Corneille et la dialectique du héros* (Paris: Gallimard, 1963); Robert J. Nelson, *Corneille: His Heroes and Their Worlds* (Philadelphia: University of Pennsylvania Press, 1963).

ing his plays from the perspective of dramatic language.[3] Perhaps this new focus will help us again to respond to Corneille's theater as did his seventeenth-century *amateurs*, not for its moral content, but for, in Mme de Sévigné's words, "ces tirades ... qui font frissonner."[4] However, Corneille's rhetoric involves more than the art of producing delicious shudders in the audience. Rhetoric is not merely a matter of technique — I. A. Richard's "usual postcard's worth of common sense" (7) — but of vision as well. Corneille's theater is a particularly striking example of the rhetorical vision which characterizes early Baroque drama in general. This chapter will treat works from Corneille's "rhetorical" period, roughly 1625 to 1650. Through an analysis of rhetorical language in Corneille, I will examine the broader import of Baroque rhetoric in its relation to truth, emotion and dramatic form. Further, the study of these rhetorical texts has led me to confront problems inherent in all rhetorical discourse. Interpretation and rhetoric exist in an uneasy dialectic, and this interpretive effort has revealed both the elusiveness of rhetoric and the limits of interpretation itself.

To clarify the view of rhetoric put forward here, it is helpful to make a preliminary distinction between two linguistic functions. In terms that the classical age would have understood very well, language can be seen as either analytical or rhetorical.[5] Analytical language is the servant of truth: its function, to efface itself and follow the contours of reality as closely as possible. This analytical function represents the ideal of scientists, philosophers and critics. Rhetoric, on the other hand, is not communicative, but combative: its function, to fight the offensive and defensive battles of the self. The rhetorical vision of life "begins with the centrality of language. It conceives reality as fundamentally dramatic, man as fundamentally a role player... Rhetorical man is an actor" (Lanham 4). And rhetorical speech is fundamentally an action — a *power play*. It refers not to an internal or

[3] See Sharon Harwood, *Rhetoric in the Tragedies of Corneille* (Ann Arbor: University Microfilms, 1977). One should also credit the work of Jean Boorsch, and particularly his "Remarques sur la technique dramatique de Corneille," *Yale Romanic Studies* 18 (1941) 101-62, as a forerunner of contemporary studies.

[4] Letter to Mme de Grignan, Wednesday, 16 March 1672, in Mme de Sévigné, *Correspondance* (Paris: Gallimard, 1972) 1459.

[5] In *The Motives of Eloquence*, R. Lanham makes a similar distinction between "rhetorical" and "serious" language. With all respect for his work, I prefer the term "analytical," which avoids certain ambiguities. Rhetoric has its own seriousness.

external (or eternal) truth, but to the will of the speaker, who satisfies his own desires by playing upon the desires of others. According to Louis Marin: "Language is representation and power. Discourse is structural strategy of desire and will, a social will, an epistemological desire as well" ("Puss in Boots" 62). Rhetorical discourse, with its referent to a desirous, role-playing self rather than to a reality "out there," stands in opposition to both the common-sense and the philosophical notion of what language should do: tell the truth about ourselves and the world.

So it is not surprising that, according to Chaim Perleman, "Relations between rhetoric and Philosophy have always been bad" (1). Rhetoric has been calumnied since Plato, in the *Phaedrus*, rejected it as a false discourse and put in its place dialectic, or the alleged discourse of truth. That the argument of the *Phaedrus* is in itself a brilliantly constructed rhetorical strategy is one of the many paradoxes surrounding this prickly subject. The word "rhetoric" retains its ambivalence today: for example, the phrase "campaign rhetoric" always refers to the discourse of one's opponents, never to one's own. Rhetoric, philosophically on the defensive, reacts by allying itself to truth.

In classical Europe the status of rhetoric was equally ambiguous. On the one hand, the classical age was a great era of eloquence. Treatises on rhetoric abounded, in both Latin and vernacular languages, and the art of speaking was regularly taught in the schools. (Until recent times the final year of the French *lycée* was called the *classe de rhétorique*.) The primary aim of rhetorical training in the seventeenth century was practical: one studied the art of persuasion in order to succeed in the pulpit, at the bar, or in everyday social situations. But despite its practical utility, even its popularity, rhetoric was never really respectable. Authors of rhetorical treatises of the period reacted by denying any real opposition between persuasive and philosophical discourse. Thus, according to Le Gras, an orator must be a virtuous man, because rhetoric gives rules for treating both sides of a subject (2-3). In this way rhetoric is reduced to a linguistic play on the surface of the real, and the discourse of truth becomes the only "true" discourse. With the interesting exception of Pascal, one rarely finds in classical theory a discussion of the philosophical status of rhetoric conceived as qualitatively different from analytic discourse. And yet it is possible to view rhetoric in its own light, not just as a shadow of truth; and despite critical denials, some classical writers operate in a chiefly rhetorical mode.

Corneille is such a writer. Within the general continuum from the rhetorical to the analytical, his language represents a *cas-limite*.[6] Despite appearances, it is basically rhetorical and only secondarily analytical. In Corneille's work, analysis is the servant of rhetoric. The so-called "Cartesian" techniques of distinction, limitation, categorization, and their stylistic corollaries (antithesis, epithet, metonymy, sententia, etc.) serve not to define an objective or even a subjective truth, but to codify and legitimize the assertions of the speaker. Cornelian *sentences*, instead of reflecting traditional wisdom, often seem made to measure for a specific occasion.[7] Thus, in *Le Cid*, when Rodrigue says to the Count: "A qui venge son père il n'est rien d'impossible" (II.2.417), it is hard to take this statement for a general moral law. To the Cornelian hero, words, like acts, are arms to be deployed in the ongoing battle of the self.

I would go even further. On the seventeenth-century stage, where physical gesture is circumscribed by propriety as well as practicality, words not only stand for deeds; they act in their own right. *Parler*, writes l'abbé d'Aubignac, *c'est agir*. And he goes on to state in an important passage: "Les plaintes d'Emilie de M. Corneille sont *l'action* d'une fille affligée qui demande justice ..." (282). Amplifying d'Aubignac's statement, Corneille writes in his *Premier discours*: "les actions sont l'âme de la tragédie, où l'on ne doit parler qu'en agissant et pour agir" (Marty-Laveaux I.39). The English word "act," both serious and theatrical, with its twin senses of accomplishment and play, comes closer than the French to Corneille's practice: not only *parler*, but *jouer, c'est agir*.

Corneille's particular mode of *parole-jeu-action* is already salient in his early comedies and particularly in *L'Illusion comique*, a play which celebrates the power of theater and of language. Critics have traditionally found little common ground between *L'Illusion* and Corneille's other works. According to François Lasserre, "C'est d'ailleurs un Corneille inconnu du public qui se révèle dans *L'Illusion*, tellement inconnu que les spectateurs ne peuvent pas rejoindre, à partir de cette nouvelle expérience, les présentations traditionnelles de son oeuvre" ("Réflexion sur le théâtre" 263). Maurice Rat, editor of the Garnier edition of Corneille, seems to reflect the traditional view when he writes

[6] I have omitted from consideration at this point "purely" poetic and religious discourse, whose standards do not apply in Corneille.

[7] See William L. Schwartz and Clarence B. Olsen, *The Sententiae in the Dramas of Corneille* (Stanford: Stanford University Press, 1939).

of *L'Illusion*: "[elle] vaut surtout par la fantaisie de l'illusion et par le style" (*Oeuvres choisies* 547). But M. Rat's disparaging judgment actually focuses attention on the central issue of the play: the workings of the theatrical imagination.[8] After exploring this aspect of Cornelian art, I will attempt to show that in his work, illusion and rhetoric are inseparable.

Corneille's notion of dramatic illusion is a complex one. As M. J. Muratore has observed, it points in the opposing directions of theatricality and verisimilitude (14-16). When in I.2, Alcandre proposes to call forth the specter of Clindor "sous une illusion," the word signifies mimesis, esthetic representation. Pridamant's use of the word *portrait* reinforces this sense: "Le portrait de celui que je cherche en tous lieux, / Pourrait-il, par sa vue, épouvanter mes yeux?" (I.2.155-56).[9] Thus, one project of the play becomes clear: through "des miracles de l'art" (I.1.88), Alcandre will create an illusion of reality before our eyes.

But other meanings also apply. According to Furetière, the first sense of illusion is deception: *fausse apparence* or *feinte*. Corneille also uses the word in this sense. At the same time he projects his theatrical illusion, he takes us behind the scenes to reveal how the illusion works, and to reveal it *as* illusion. Corneille creates a "frame" for his play, in which Alcandre, with his omniscience and magical powers of creation, represents the author-director. The "spectres pareils à des corps animés" (I.2.152) stand for both the characters, disembodied figments of the author's imagination, and the actors, who lose their names, their identity, their very being, when they take on a dramatic role. Most important, Pridamant represents the audience as it undergoes a theatrical initiation. By showing what it means to be an author or an actor, Corneille above all shows us how to be spectators. From the beginning, Alcandre carefully instructs Pridamant in the art of play-going. He is told, for example, that the figures he will see are *fantômes vains* ("it's only a play"). Alcandre's mysterious injunction not to leave the cavern (II.1.216-17) may also be interpreted in

[8] As Lasserre points out, Corneille's interest in illusion is not philosophic but dramatic: "Corneille en effet n'a pas été intéressé dans ce thème par des spéculations évasives sur l'irréalité de la vie, etc. ..., mais par la mise en place d'un schéma de fonctionnement concret, et par les règles sociologiques du microcosme théâtral" ("Avant *L'Illusion*" 730).

[9] Quotations from Corneille's plays generally refer to *Théâtre complet*, ed. Maurice Rat (Paris: Garnier, 1960), vols. I and II. Quotations from other editions will be indicated in parentheses by editor, as will references to Rat in cases of possible ambiguity.

this sense. The gap between audience and stage, reality and representation, cannot be bridged by flesh-and-blood mortals. Crossing the footlights not only destroys the dramatic illusion but causes the interloper psychic discomfort.

When Pridamant, ignoring Alcandre's counsel, repeatedly takes dramatic illusion for reality, he suffers the emotional consequences. At the end of act II, we find the following exchange:

> ALCANDRE. Le coeur vous bat un peu.
> PRIDAMANT. Je crains cette menace.
> ALCANDRE. Lyse aime trop Clindor pour causer sa disgrâce.
> (II.10.621-22)

At the close of act III, Pridamant becomes even more agitated;

> PRIDAMANT. Hélas! mon fils est mort.
> ALCANDRE. Que vous avez d'alarmes!
> PRIDAMANT. Ne lui refusez point le secours de vos charmes.
> ALCANDRE. Un peu de patience, et, sans un tel secours,
> Vous le verrez bientôt heureux en ses amours.
> (III.12.985-88)

The joke is on Pridamant, who fears for the life of a ghost. Within the fictional plot, a parallel trick is played on Clindor himself, who believes he will be killed, while the other characters, and the audience, know differently. The eloquent language of his prison monologue (IV.7) is undercut by this comic contrast: "Trompeur trop obligeant! tu disais bien vraiment / Que je mourrais de nuit, mais de contentement" (IV.9.1303-04).

By these means, Corneille establishes a distance between the novice play-goers like Pridamant, who take illusion for truth, and the theatrical connoisseurs who can see through such tricks... perhaps. For Corneille has reserved a particularly ingenious theatrical imposture for the final act. In a double illusion, the "phantoms" of Lyse and Clindor are made to represent actors playing roles in a tragedy. In order to confuse things still further, Corneille draws parallels between the lives of the original characters and the plot of the tragedy they are performing. Clindor, sadly fickle in III.6, seems to have fallen back into his old ways in V.4; and the jealous Adraste, unable to kill Clindor in III.11, appears to finish the job successfully two acts later. Some members of the audience, taken in by this ploy, may come to share the anxieties of Pridamant, thereby losing the quasi-detachment that defines the theatrical experience. But in the end, all is *jeu*; and despite Alcandre's warnings, no one dies, either on stage or off. Thus, the state of mind fostered by *L'Illusion* is not the standard suspension of disbelief, but a simultaneous belief and disbelief, illusion and disillusion. Corneille has indeed "framed" his play, but unlike the proscenium arch which sets the stage apart from the hall and the world, Corneille's construction unites the three in a new alliance, held together not merely by dramatic illusion — *le fard et l'artifice du langage* — but by dramatic power.

In *L'Illusion*, then, the author and his representative Alcandre manipulate both actors and audience at will. They are, by Aristotelian standards, "successful" characters who advance the action through words and deeds. Yet Matamore, *L'Illusion*'s most felicitous creation, does nothing of the kind. As Robert Garapon puts it, "Le rôle de Matamore repose tout entier sur une autonomie du langage par rapport à l'action (et donc à l'utilité) qui est la définition même de la fantaisie verbale" (*Fantaisie* 10). When Matamore speaks, words go one way, things another. Certain of his speeches justify their existence through linguistic verve alone:

> Je te donne le choix de trois ou quatre morts:
> Je vais, d'un coup de poing, te briser comme verre,
> Ou t'enfoncer tout vif au centre de la terre,
> Ou te fendre en dix parts d'un seul coup de revers,
> Ou te jeter si haut au-dessus des éclairs,
> Que tu sois dévoré des feux élémentaires. (III.9.924-29)

But the text invites us to interpret *fantaisie* in a different sense, more in keeping with the previous discussion. Matamore has been taken over by his own language to the point that illusion has become delusion. The first lines Clindor addresses to him already suggest that Matamore is not in an ordinary state of mind: "Quoi! monsieur, vous rêvez!" (II.1.221). And Matamore agrees: "Il est vrai que je rêve, et ne saurais résoudre / Lequel je dois des deux le premier mettre en poudre, / Du grand sophi de Perse, ou bien du grand mogor" (225-27). These extravagant claims are presented not just as boastful, but insane: in acts II and III, he is called *fou* by at least four different characters. Lyse poetically dubs him "ce prince des fous" (II.8.568). Ironically, when Géronte unceremoniously tries to get rid of a man he considers mad, Matamore comments: "Il a perdu le sens, de me parler ainsi" (III.3.724). But the most revealing depiction is probably Adraste's: "Un fanfaron plus fou que son discours n'est vain" (II.7.540). In Matamore's speeches, vain rhetoric and madness are equated.

Like the classic maniac, Matamore constantly tries to shore up his illusory vision against the inexorable pressures of real existence. Finding this task too much to handle alone, he often calls on outside aid from Clindor. For example, Matamore asks Isabelle: "... souffrez cependant / Une heure d'entretien de ce cher confident, / Qui, comme de ma vie il sait toute l'histoire, / Vous fera voir sur qui vous avez la victoire" (II.5.471-74). Clindor even "remembers" certain of Matamore's exploits that his master has himself forgotten (II.5.456-57). In III.3, like an actor who has "dried up," he asks Clindor to second him against a threatening Oronte: "Dis-lui ce que j'ai fait en mille et mille lieux" (731). Matamore, his vein of fantasy temporarily exhausted, leaves it up to Clindor to fill in the details.

Even after he has openly claimed Isabelle for himself, Clindor continues to play his habitual role, picking up Matamore's cues:

> MATAMORE. Je te la veux donner pour prix de tes services;
> Plains-toi dorénavant d'avoir un maître ingrat!
> CLINDOR. A ce rare présent, d'aise le coeur me bat.
> Protecteur des grands rois, guerrier trop magnanime,
> Puisse tout l'univers bruire de votre estime! (III.10.954-58)

This is, of course, ironic; but it allows Matamore to maintain his protective fantasy until the end. And until the end, Clindor holds verbal sway over his master. Like the picaresque heroes to whom Corneille compares him (I.3.185), Clindor lives by his wits, which means by his words: "Il sait avec adresse, *en portant les paroles*, / De la vaillante dupe attraper les pistoles" (197-98) — *et la maîtresse.*

This allusion to the Spanish comic novel suggests another fictional parallel for Corneille's *fou*. Not only is he identified with the farcical tradition of the *capitán*, the Rodomont; he also brings to mind that archetypal literary lunatic, Don Quixote. Like Matamore, Quixote mistakes words for things, fiction for reality. Like Matamore's, his delusion is treated in a parodic, mock-heroic mode. But there is at least one essential difference between them. Quixote, while falsely taking windmills for giants, is truly brave; Matamore only pretends to be, and very unsuccessfully at that. This makes one wonder whether Matamore's folly is fully *folie* — whether he is entirely the dupe of

Clindor's machinations or his own delusions. In his effort to maintain the persona he has created, Matamore can display a self-conscious ingenuity beyond the reach of the "normal" maniac. For example, when Clindor suggests he face Adraste instead of running away ("Cessez d'être charmant, et faites-vous terrible") Matamore replies:

> Mais tu n'en prévois pas l'accident infaillible:
> Je ne saurais me faire effroyable à demi;
> Je tuerais ma maîtresse avec mon ennemi. (III.3.342-45)

One wonders who is fooling whom.

Again, when Matamore is discovered hiding in Isabelle's attic, the following exchange ensues:

> MATAMORE. Pour conserver une dame aussi belle,
> Au plus haut du logis j'ai fait la sentinelle...
> LYSE. C'est-à-dire, en deux mots,
> Que la peur l'enfermait dans la chambre aux fagots.
> MATAMORE. La peur?
> LYSE. Oui, vous tremblez; la vôtre est sans égale.
> MATAMORE. Parce qu'elle a bon pas, j'en fais mon Bucéphale;
> Lorsque je la domptai, je lui fis cette loi;
> Et depuis, quand je marche, elle tremble sous moi. (IV.4.1157-64)

This persiflage has none of the obsessive intensity associated with madness — even the comic madness of a Harpagon. It is rather as though Corneille lets Matamore step out of his role momentarily — remove his mask and play with it.

Matamore's one soliloquy displays similar shifts between reality and illusion, mask and madness. Alone, he frankly expresses his fears. Every sound, every breath of wind is transformed by his imagination into a hidden enemy:

> Les voilà, sauvons-nous. Non, je ne vois personne.
> Avançons hardiment. Tout le corps me frissonne.
> Je les entends, fuyons. Le vent faisait ce bruit. (III.7.861-63)

However, Matamore's exaggerated terrors do have a real basis:

> Ces diables de valets me mettent bien en peine.
> De deux mille ans et plus, je ne tremblai si fort. (866-68)

His cowardice once disclosed, he immediately tries to cover it with heroic words:

> Car j'aime mieux mourir que leur donner bataille,
> Et profaner mon bras contre cette canaille. (869-70)

Frightened again, this time by real intruders, he resolves on flight: "J'ai le pied pour le moins aussi bon que l'épée" (874). However, when he discovers that the two figures are not Géronte's valets but Isabelle and Clindor, he once again takes up his comic pretensions to glory:

> Destin, qu'à ma valeur tu te montres contraire!...
> C'est ma reine elle-même, avec mon secrétaire! (877-78)

Matamore's final exit in IV.4 is prepared in a similar way. He happily discourses on mythical topics until Isabelle threatens him with a real beating:

> ISABELLE. Lyse, fais-moi sortir les valets de mon père.
> MATAMORE. Un sot les attendrait. (1190-91)

Matamore, like Hamlet, is only mad north-west; he may wander into the realm of verbal fantasy, but he knows when it is time to stop talking and start running.

This examination of Matamore's speech reveals how Corneille limits and rationalizes the "Baroque madness" critics sometimes ascribe to plays of the period.[10] His flights of fancy never achieve the verbal autonomy Foucault ascribes to Cervantes' language: "La vérité de Don Quichotte, elle n'est pas dans le rapport des mots au monde, mais dans cette mince et constante relation que les marques verbales tissent d'elles-mêmes à elles-mêmes" (*Les Mots* 62). Unlike Don Quixote's, the basis of Matamore's discourse is neither illusion nor madness, but self-protection. Matamore does not know, or care, how words relate to the world or to each other; what counts is how they relate to *him*. Not a very Quixotic attitude, but a very Cornelian one.

This point brings us from free-floating fantasy back to earth — and to rhetoric. Cornelian characters, as good rhetoricians, use speech neither to express nor to hide thought but to get what they want from other people. As Lasserre puts it, "Chaque personnage cherche à créer chez les autres une inclination qui les fasse agir dans le sens qu'il souhaite" ("Avant *L'Illusion*" 713). Matamore is no exception. Since he fails in his aim, he is comic; if he had succeeded, he would have been

[10] Jean Rousset, in *La Littérature de l'âge baroque en France* (Paris: Corti, 1954), formulated categories of the "Baroque" which had great influence on ensuing criticism.

heroic. In fact, he already speaks a hero's language. *L'Illusion* is a treasure-trove of Cornelian rhetoric: the longer one looks, the more lines one unearths which will resurface in Corneille's "serious" plays. *Le Cid* and *L'Illusion*, produced within less than a year of each other, contain nearly interchangeable expressions:

> *Le seul bruit de mon nom* renverse les murailles,
> (*L'Illusion*: Matamore, II.2.233)
>
> *Mon nom* sert de rempart à toute la Castille:
> (*Le Cid*: Le Comte, I.3.198)
>
> Oui; tout autre que moi
> *Au seul bruit de ton nom* pourrait trembler d'effroi,
> (*Le Cid*: Rodrigue, II.2.411-12)
>
> ... il est vaillant lui-même;
> *Il commandait sous moi*:
> (*L'Illusion*: Matamore, III.10.965-66)
>
> Je vous ai vu combattre et *commander sous moi*:
> *Le Cid*: Don Diègue, I.3.208)

The resemblance is disconcerting. Divorced from its context, farcical hyberbole looks a lot like heroic "hype"; and if the names were left out, it would be hard to tell which lines were spoken by the false Moor-killer (Matamore), which by the real. But the identity goes deeper. The mock-heroic is more than a mirror-image of the heroic, Matamore more than a comic inversion of Rodrigue; he *is* Rodrigue, a Rodrigue *manqué*. Matamore's voluntarism, his craving to conquer the world and himself through words, are as strong as any hero's. But when he fails in his heroic ambition, his language turns parodically against itself:

> Je te le dis encor, ne sois plus en alarme:
> Quand je veux, j'épouvante; et quand je veux, je charme;
> Et, selon qu'il me plaît, je remplis tour à tour
> Les hommes de terreur, et les femmes d'amour. (II.2.257-60)

Thus, *L'Illusion*, like *Le Cid*, explores rhetoric's power to work one's will on the world. But in *L'Illusion*, rhetorical power, if not rhetorical play, remains firmly in the hands of the author, and the only real winner is theater itself. As Pridamant states in the final scene:

> Il est vrai que d'abord mon âme s'est émue:
> J'ai cru la comédie au point où je l'ai vue;
> J'en ignorais l'éclat, l'utilité, l'appas,

> Et la blâmais ainsi, ne le [sic] connaissant pas;
> Mais, depuis vos discours, mon coeur plein d'allégresse
> A banni cette erreur avecque sa tristesse. (V.5.1673-78)

Having transformed Pridamant into the ideal spectator, Alcandre can gracefully conclude: "J'ai pris ma récompense en vous faisant plaisir" (V.5.1684). As Corneille asserts, in accord with his contemporaries, the primary esthetic aim is to please; "selon Aristote, le seul but de la póesie dramatique soit de plaire aux spectateurs ..." (*Writings on the Theatre* 1). But the author-magician achieves his overall objectives somewhat at the characters' expense. Even the central figures, Isabelle and Clindor, are moved around like marionettes. They are not actors in the full sense, but phantoms of actors whose deeds never quite coincide with their words. When that convergence occurs, Cornelian rhetoric *about* drama will yield the stage to rhetorical drama.

In *Le Cid*, the rhetorical act deploys itself freely and fully. With acrobatic ease, Corneille sidesteps moral conflicts which might threaten the balance of his play. Dramatic tension in *Le Cid* arises from the conflict not of values, but of wills; the surface strife and argumentation overlay a basic accord. At the end of II.2, as the Count and Rodrigue set off for their duel, the former is able to say in complete moral harmony with his challenger: "Viens, tu fais ton devoir" (441). Even the *stances du Cid* (I.6), which appear to record a profound struggle, fail to raise serious questions of right and wrong. Despite the symmetry of its formal oppositions, and the ingenious psychological interpretations it has evoked,[11] Rodrigue's famous monologue does not constitute a moral debate. From the very start, the balance is tipped to one side. After a first moment of shock ("Je demeure immobile, et mon âme abattue / Cède au coup qui me tue" [I.6.295-96]), Rodrigue begins to deliberate with himself: "Réduit au triste choix ou de trahir ma flamme, / Ou de vivre en infâme, / Des deux côtés mon mal est infini" (305-07). But, in fact, Rodrigue is not suspended between deux *infinis*, as he claims, because *infâme* falls heavier on the

[11] See the subtle analysis of Doubrovsky (*Dialectique du héros* 98-105). My analysis of rhetoric in the *stances* takes a somewhat different approach from Sharon Harwood's in "Logic and Emotion: The Structure of Orations and the Uses of Rhetorical Figures in Corneille," *PFSCL* 3 (1975) 27-28. On the other hand, I am in close agreement with the study of Milorad Margitic, "Texte et sous-texte chez Corneille: une lecture des Stances de Rodrigue," *Saggi e Ricercche di Letterature Francese* 16 (1977) 199-212.

moral scales than *flamme*. This unequal weighting of epithets gradually becomes more pronounced in the course of the third *strophe*:

> Noble et dure contrainte, aimable tyrannie,
> Tous mes plaisirs sont morts, ou ma gloire ternie.
> L'un me rend malheureux, l'autre indigne du jour. (312-14)

If we extract the value-bearing terms from this *strophe*, a pattern emerges as in figure 4. The terms Rodrigue uses eliminate any possibility of moral ambiguity: if it is bad to be *malheureux*, it is inarguably worse to be *indigne du jour*.

Devoir		Amour
noble	←------→	aimable
dure contrainte	←------→	tyrannie
plaisirs morts	←------→	gloire ternie
malheureux	←------→	indigne du jour

Figure 4

In the last three *strophes* of *stances* (321-50), the stylistic pattern changes as Rodrigue, with a series of first-person imperatives (*allons mon âme... allons mon bras... courons... ne soyons plus*), exhorts himself to action. These *-ons* imperatives and their accompanying metonymies (*âme*, *bras*) are a sign, in the Cornelian style, of the speaker's attempt to choose a position through which his will can assert itself. *Prenons parti*, *mon âme*, says Sabine in *Horace* (III.1.711). Rodrigue *prend parti* by the dramatic means of "trying out" two solutions, by hearing himself express them in words. The first option, at the end of *strophe* three, is suicide: "Allons, mon âme; et puisqu'il faut mourir / Mourons du moins sans offenser Chimène" (329-30). But, as if on cue, the paronomasia *mourir/Mourons* sets off a rhetorical avalanche: "Mourir sans tirer ma raison! / Rechercher un trépas si mortel à ma gloire, / Endurer que l'Espagne impute à ma mémoire / D'avoir mal soutenu l'honneur de ma maison!" (331-34). This series of exclamations does not call into question the moral justification of suicide ("whether 'tis nobler in the mind"), but its effect on others, its heroic efficacy: "Que dira-t-on de lui?" as Chimène will ask later (II.4.488). Sensitive to this *qu'en dira-t-on*, Rodrigue rejects suicide in favor of honor: "Allons, mon bras, sauvons du moins l'honneur" (339). Thus, through the dramatic, generative power of words, a course of action, which was never seriously in doubt, is formally set forth. In the final *strophe*, this *prise de position* completed, Rodrigue's rhetoric undergoes a hardening process. The antithetical balances no longer obtain, not even in appearance: "Je dois tout à mon père avant qu'à ma maîtresse" (342). Language has openly coincided with purpose. This outcome has been inscribed from the beginning in the rhetorical intentionality of the *stances*: like a Platonic dialogue, Rodrigue's monologue has only the appearance of debate.

If the *stances* are not primarily moral or psychological analysis, not an attempt to portray a soul torn between Love and Duty, what, then, is their function? First, they generate a process of dramatic feedback. By hearing his own words and reacting to them as his own audience, Rodrigue gets himself back into the heroic role after his momentary dejection: "oui, mon esprit s'était déçu" (341). As a *rhetor*, a creature of the publicly spoken word, Rodrigue can find and reinforce his own values only by speaking them: "making up his mind" is equivalent to, and indistinguishable from, stating his case.[12]

More important, this language of apparent deliberation involves the audience in the action, making Rodrigue an object of sympathy and enlisting support for his future acts. Given the same basic situation, one can imagine quite a different play in which killing a loved one's relatives would remain morally questionable: Corneille will write this play in *Horace*. In *Le Cid*, however, the essential values of the warrior caste remain unquestioned. This tacit agreement on values is a necessary precondition for rhetorical "play" to proceed freely.

Rodrigue, as befits the dynamic new hero, is the best rhetorical player of the lot. He couples great linguistic virtuosity with equally great control. Thus, for example, in his *tête-à-tête* with Chimène (III.4), his blood-stained sword in hand, he adopts the formal tones of the respectful lover: "Eh bien! sans vous donner la peine de poursuivre, / Assurez-vous l'honneur de m'empêcher de vivre" (849-50). His polite formulas (*sans vous donner la peine*, *assurez-vous l'honneur*) and elaborate periphrase for *tuer* (*empêcher de vivre*) stand in ironic opposition to the outrageous nature of his suggestion. His speech also contrasts with the ordinary tone of conversation between the two lovers, who are normally on *tu-toi*, Rodrigue-Chimène terms. This studied combination of formality with violence breaks down Chimène's guard and forces her confession of love.

[12] See Lanham 134: "Feelings are not real until played. Drama, ceremony is always needed to authenticate experience."

The potential violence of this scene never even threatens to become real; it always remains contained in the rhetorical fabric. As Chimène explains to Rodrigue, and as he already knows, it is not a woman's role to take vengeance directly:

> Va, je suis ta partie, et non pas ton bourreau.
> Si tu m'offres ta tête, est-ce à moi de la prendre?
> Je la dois attaquer, mais tu dois la défendre;
> C'est d'un autre que toi qu'il me faut l'obtenir,
> Et je dois te poursuivre, et non pas te punir. (940-44)

Using a legal vocabulary well suited to the rhetorical situation, Chimène maintains that her duty is to prosecute, not execute, to act not physically, but verbally. Upon reflection, we realize that Rodrigue is in no real danger. But Corneille gives us no time to reflect. At the moment of dramatic action, the rhetorical ploy works both on Chimène (Rodrigue's audience) and on us (Corneille's audience).

Sacrificial victim on love's altar is only one of Rodrigue's roles. In act IV, he shows his rhetorical talents in quite a different context. At the beginning of scene 3, the King has just named him Cid and protector of Castille. But he does not fall into the trap of excessive arrogance — unlike Chimène's father, who said: "Tout l'Etat périra, s'il faut que je périsse" (II.1.378). Instead, Rodrigue tells Don Fernand what a king wants to hear:

> Je sais trop que je dois au bien de votre empire
> Et le sang qui m'anime, et l'air que je respire;
> Et quand je les perdrai pour un si digne objet,
> Je ferai seulement le devoir d'un sujet. (IV.3.1233-36)

Rodrigue plays to win and will adopt whatever means necessary to accomplish his ends. In order to conquer the king as he has conquered his enemies, he will play the role of humble subject. He does not make the mistake of identifying with his own language.

Thanks in large part to this verbal flexibility, Rodrigue is the only character in the play who fully achieves his aims. Chimène is less successful, but, then, her position is more difficult. It is her father who has been killed, and the problems arising from his death cannot be resolved by mere deliberation. Nevertheless, Chimène follows the same rhetorical imperative as Rodrigue to make the best case possible out of the material at hand. Upon learning of the dispute between Rodrigue and her father, Chimène had expressed anxiety and uncertainty about the future: "Je sens couler des pleurs que je veux retenir; /

Le passé me tourmente, et je crains l'avenir" (II.3.479-80). But none of this uncertainty shows in II.8, Chimène's *grande scène*, where she plays to the hilt the role of the injured daughter seeking revenge. Her forensic rhetoric exemplifies the symbiotic relation between emotion and public discourse that is peculiar to Corneille's drama.

At the beginning of her long speech, Chimène still has before her eyes the violent image of her father's death. "Sire, mon père est mort; mes yeux ont vu son sang" (359). But the rhetorical faculty immediately takes over: "Couler à gros bouillons de son généreux flanc." It is the epithet *généreux* that makes the transition from recital or oration. It "generates," in fact, the first rhetorical movement, built on the anaphora *ce sang qui...*:

> Ce sang qui tant de fois garantit vos murailles,
> Ce sang qui tant de fois vous gagna des batailles,
> Ce sang qui tout sorti fume encor de courroux
> De se voir répandu pour d'autres que pour vous ... (661-64)

The word *sang* conveys both Chimène's personal horror at the remembered sight of her father's blood and the public significance of his life and death. In the Baroque personification, "Ce sang qui tout sorti fume encor de courroux," personal and public meanings fuse together: *sang*, metonymic emblem for the life-force of the hero, also represents metaphorically the life-blood of the state, shed needlessly in a private cause.

After this first climax, Chimène is overcome by grief: "Sire, la voix me manque à ce récit funeste; / Mes pleurs et mes soupirs vous diront mieux le reste" (669-70). But, significantly, she uses her very grief rhetorically to further her argument in a way reminiscent of Mark Antony's funeral oration in *Julius Caesar*: "Bear with me; My heart is in the coffin there with Caesar, / and I must pause till it come back to me." The Shakespearean affinity reappears in the second half of Chimène's speech:

> CHIMENE. Son sang sur la poussière écrivait mon devoir;
> Ou plutôt sa valeur en cet état réduite
> Me parlait par sa plaie, et hâtait ma poursuite;
> Et, pour se faire entendre au plus juste des rois,
> Par cette triste bouche elle empruntait ma voix. (676-80)

> ANTONY. I tell you that which you yourselves do know;
> Show you sweet Caesar's wounds, poor poor dumb mouths,
> And bid them speak for me. (*Julius Caesar* III.2.220-22)

There is in Antony's rhetoric a "democratic" pretense to plain speaking which Chimène disdains to make; unlike Shakespeare's Romans, Corneille's Spaniards never feel the need to disguise *l'art de bien parler*.[13] In both speeches, however, the orators "publicize" their grief by transforming it dramatically: the speaker's grieving voice becomes the voice of the victim seeking justice. Personal emotion is objectified and rendered more powerful through identification with a public cause.[14]

The peroration of Chimène's speech completes the fusion of private feeling to public oratory. Chimène concludes her argument with what can aptly be called a rhetorical flight:

> Immolez, non à moi, mais à votre couronne,
> Mais à votre grandeur, mais à votre personne;
> Immolez, dis-je, sire, au bien de tout l'Etat
> Tout ce qu'enorgueillit un si haut attentat. (693-96)

The phrase *mais à votre...* , like *ce sang qui...* , emphasizes the public consequences of the Count's death. And yet it is Chimène's emotional presence which impels the language on to a climax: "Immolez, *dis-je...*" Fueled by emotion, the rhetoric becomes self-energizing. To use an aerospace metaphor, escape velocity is reached and the discourse "takes off," carrying away with it both speaker and audience.

As an example of rhetorical power, Chimène's speech is hard to surpass; as a practical incitement to violence, it is a failure. From the beginning, Don Fernand refuses to take it "seriously" as rhetoric — as a spur to action — and persists in seeing it only as an expression of grief: *une plainte*. His condescendingly paternalistic statements, such as "Prends du repos, ma fille, et calme tes douleurs" (739), exasperate Chimène by their obtuseness: "M'ordonner du repos, c'est croître mes malheurs" (740).

Thrown back on her own resources at the beginning of act III, Chimène reformulates her rhetorical stance. Her persistent love for Rodrigue, instead of a shameful weakness, becomes a proof of strength as she continues to seek his destruction. Chimène proclaims to Elvire in III.3: "Mais, en ce dur combat de colère et de flamme, / Il

[13] Chimène's speech, in fact, is an elegant adaptation of the Spanish original: Que me habló / Por la boca de la herida. / Y escrivió / Con sangre mi obligación (Couton 795, 825).

[14] In "Hand, Heart and Mind: The Complexity of the Heroic Quest in *Le Cid*," *PMLA* 91 (1976) 44-53, William Goode discusses this question from a more strictly psychological perspective than mine.

déchire mon coeur sans partager mon âme ... / Je cours sans balancer où mon honneur m'oblige" (817-18, 821). These lines vie with and surpass the conclusion of Rodrigue's *stances*, "tout honteux d'avoir tant balancé." Although Chimène has no soliloquy, the scenes with her *confidante* serve the same function: to create a self-image she can impose upon the world. Act III.4 is the performance for which the preceding scenes served as rehearsal. In this duet with Rodrigue, Chimène literally turns her predicament into *gloire*. Her involuntary confession of love in this scene represents a rhetorical victory for Rodrigue; and yet, once she has made it, she immediately starts transforming it from a source of shame into a proof of virtue:

RODRIGUE. Crains-tu si peu le blâme, et si peu les faux bruits?
Quand on saura mon crime, et que ta flamme dure,
Que ne publieront point l'envie et l'imposture? (964-66)
CHIMENE. Elle [ma renommée] éclate bien mieux en te laissant la vie;
Et je veux que la voix de la plus noire envie
Elève au ciel ma gloire et plaigne mes ennuis,
Sachant que je t'adore et que je te poursuis. (969-72)

Chimène resolutely grasps both horns of her dilemma, finding in its very duality a proof of her uniqueness. *Ce qui fait frissonner*, in Mme de Sévigné's terms, is this verbal audacity in turning apparent weakness into strength. Through the rhetorical energy of her language — subjunctives, superlatives, antitheses — she willfully opposes her own self-definition to the conventional wisdom of society. Her rhetoric is the instrument of her freedom.

This freedom, however, is never realized. Chimène's partial failure in this respect is more telling than Rodrigue's total success, because it reveals both the power and the limits of Cornelian rhetoric. Chimène's language is indeed free and autonomous, but its very autonomy is a two-edged sword: with words, she can define herself as she wishes, but she cannot change the course of events around her. This limitation ensues in part from the political structure of the play: Rodrigue, the new public hero, cannot succumb to a private vengeance. By defeating the Moors, Rodrigue effectively destroys Chimène's argument, in II.8, that he is the enemy of royal authority. After Rodrigue's victory, Chimène stands alone, in splendid isolation from the common cause: *autre que moi*, she claims with bitter pride, *n'a droit de soupirer* (1147). On another level, however, the separation of words from events and the substitution of words for deeds, intrinsic to Chimène's language, are basic premises of Corneille's rhetorical vision.

As we will see, this vision finds its fullest expression in *Nicomède*, where the hero works his will through words alone. Far from his army, lured into enemy hands, Nicomède verbally converts all to his heroic cause. Yet even here, rhetorical autonomy has its limits. At a critical point, *res* and *verba* must reconnect: the *grands mots* of the heroic rhetoric must rest upon a substrate of *hauts faits*. As Nicomède himself says, valor without results (*une vertu sans effets*) is without reality (*imaginaire*).[15]

Paradoxically, then, the Cornelian hero's rhetorical freedom springs from an identity between words and truth so total that truth ceases to be at issue. Since his exploits provide a sub- or pre-text which guarantees the veracity of his words, he is on a very long verbal leash; he can say almost anything and be believed. He, not she. For the guarantee does not work for heroines. While men can both act and speak, women can only speak, a disparity which will ultimately deny Chimène heroic stature. Camille, in *Horace*, attains it as fully as a woman can, but only by getting herself killed. Since such a tragic solution would be out of place in *Le Cid*, Corneille takes care of Chimène by "shifting down" into comedy.

The intrusion of comedy into *Le Cid* causes a basic change in the epistemological premises of the play. As our study of *L'Illusion* has shown, while heroic drama rests on an implicit accord of word and deed, Cornelian comedy arises from their inconsistency. In drama, the hero is taken at his word because he draws on a store of deeds or, at least, has the potential required to perform such deeds. Just as actions in Cornelian drama constitute capital, noble race guarantees credit. The comic character, however, by definition not a *généreux*, rates no credit at all. His word is constantly tested — and found wanting. Whereas in drama, language is an authentic expression of the self — the face one has chosen to show the world — in comedy it is an illusory surface behind which lurks some psychological truth, distinct from, and opposed to, words themselves. The basic comic situation in Corneille is, thus, a testing situation in which the incongruity between words and truth is humiliatingly brought home to the speaker.

This is the kind of comic testing which Chimène undergoes in the last scenes of *Le Cid*: as Don Fernand says, "je vais l'éprouver" (IV.4.1336). To prove Chimène, he uses an untruth which, like a counter-poison, provokes a "sincere" reaction: Don Fernand announces the false news of Rodrigue's death, and Chimène faints. From the

[15] This line is a paraphrase of *Nicomède* II.3.640-41.

King's point of view, this stratagem is a success. Chimène's action (or, more accurately, *passion* — cessation of action) is taken by Don Fernand as the desired proof that, in spite of her words, she "really" loves Rodrigue. This episode replays in the comic mode the encounter between Rodrigue and Chimène (III.4) that we have already analyzed, and it is enlightening to compare the two. In both instances, the basic (and same) "truth" is known from the start: simply, Chimène loves Rodrigue. Again, in both cases, the object is not to find out the truth, but to have it declared. By his sophisticated verbal aggression in III.4, Rodrigue was able to make Chimène say what he already knew, but had to hear: "Va, je ne te hais point" (963). Don Fernand wants the same thing, but lacks the skill (and attraction) to make Chimène speak. So, like a critic, he must resort to interpretation: he decodes Chimène's fainting to mean "I love Rodrigue."

What is interesting about this incident is not the "secret" of Chimène's love, which has never been a secret to anyone, but the means used to uncover it. Under the license granted by comedy, Chimène is treated differently from the other characters; the King is able to impose on her words a single meaning. Chimène continues to assert her rhetorical freedom to define her own position, but to no avail:

> DON FERNAND. Consulte bien ton coeur; Rodrigue en est le maître.
> Et ta flamme en secret rend grâces à ton roi,
> Dont la faveur conserve un tel amant pour toi.
> CHIMENE. Pour moi! mon ennemi! l'objet de ma colère!
> L'auteur de mes malheurs! l'assassin de mon père!
> De ma juste poursuite on fait si peu de cas
> Qu'on me croit obliger en ne m'écoutant pas! (IV.5.1390-96)

The opposition here is not between truth and pretense, as Don Fernand claims, but between two concepts of truth. For Chimène, as for Corneille, truth is multi-faceted. Rodrigue is her *ennemi*, but *also* her *amant*; she must love him *and* pursue him. The epithets she chooses to further her pursuit — *ennemi*, *assassin*, *objet de ma colère* — do not tell the truth about her situation, but *a* truth, her chosen truth. The King's epithets — *coeur*, *flamme* — are equally reductive. One could say that Chimène and Fernand's speeches, taken together, come closer to the truth about Chimène than either one taken separately. But this is not the point, because Corneille's rhetoric does not seek to define *the* truth; on the contrary, the dramatic effect of the scene arises precisely from a conflict between limited rhetorical perspectives. On an epistemological level, moreover, telling the truth in a Cornelian context is not only undesirable (because undramatic), but also impossible: mortals may aspire to transcendent verities, but on earth they cling to shards of belief. The epistemological position implicit here comes close to that expressed by Pascal in his remarks on persuasion: "Quand on veut reprendre avec utilité, et montrer à un autre qu'il se trompe, il faut observer par quel côté il envisage la chose, car elle est vraie ordinairement de ce côté-là ... naturellement l'homme ne peut tout voir" (B9, L701). In comedy, as in tragedy, the central motif is that of blindness (Oedipus, Thésée, Orgon); in Cornelian theater, despite Don Fernand's efforts, we have the drama of finite vision.

Her verbal pursuit of Rodrigue once again foiled by the King, Chimène turns as a last resort to action by proxy: "Puisque vous refusez la justice à mes larmes, / Sire, permettez-moi de recourir aux armes" (1397-98). This appeal, rooted in feudal tradition, cannot be ignored easily. For a moment, comedy threatens to turn back into drama, but Fernand, maintaining his self-appointed role as father (*père de comédie*) to a rebellious daughter, insists that she marry the winner of the duel:

> CHIMENE. Quoi! sire, m'imposer une si dure loi!
> DON FERNAND. Tu t'en plains; mais ton feu, loin d'avouer ta plainte,
> Si Rodrigue est vainqueur, l'accepte sans contrainte. (1460-63)

The *tutoiement*, the reference to Chimène's *vainqueur*, and the metonymic reduction of Chimène to her *feu*, all define her as a dependent, wholly emotive being, a definition she refuses to accept.

Happily, the ending of the play brings an end to Chimène's comic humiliation and a return to the heroic world of the first three acts. Once Don Fernand has been allowed his verbal revenge, he admits, at least to some degree, the legitimacy of Chimène's complaints. Whereas earlier he had reduced her metonymically to *coeur* and *feu*, *gloire* now makes a reappearance: "Il faudrait que je fusse ennemi de ta *gloire* / Pour lui donner sitôt le prix de sa victoire" (V.7.1817-18). Thus, the threat to Chimène's integrity is shown to be perhaps the cleverest rhetorical ploy of all: the King, who appeared to be the heavy father of comedy, is now revealed merely to have been playing a role, with the same rhetorical flexibility, the same capacity to "tune his supple song" to mood and moment, as those shown by the main characters. Yet this *dénouement*, while it brings reconciliation, does not resolve the basic moral issue: whether Chimène can in conscience marry a man who killed her father. This question is not settled, but postponed, pushed out of the temporal limits of the play to make way for a brilliant finale: "Prends un an, si tu veux, pour essuyer tes larmes" (1821). The ploy of postponement, like others we have observed in the course of this study, works — at the time. It is not until after the curtain falls that we have time to reflect and to ask ourselves the perennial question, "Will Chimène *really* marry Rodrigue?" This question is a natural one, but cannot, I think, be legitimately posed about *Le Cid*. In this play, Corneille uses all his dramatic skills to transform the stage into a charmed rhetorical realm which, although repeatedly threatened, comes through all trials unbroken. Verbal behavior remains freewheeling, adapted to context; the basic elements of rhetorical discourse remain the tools of the speaker and not his masters. The characters may suffer from inner conflicts, but they manage to make use of their sufferings by dramatizing them; and, by turning suffering into play, they even come at times to enjoy it. Perhaps this is the *morale* to be drawn from a work which, despite its labelings and relabelings throughout the years, is neither *comédie* nor *tragicomédie* nor *tragédie*, but *jeu*: a brilliant dramatic illusion which continues to work its charm on theater audiences, despite nearly three and a half centuries of interpretation.

The verbal freedom that reigns so fully in *Le Cid* no longer obtains in *Horace*. Cornelian rhetoric undergoes yet another shift: from an instrument of liberation, it becomes a source of awkwardness and constraint, an awkwardness which penetrates the intimate texture of the poetry itself. Even great poets do not always write great verse, and Corneille's plays contain certain lines that critics have passed over in discreet silence. From *Le Cid*, for example, we have "J'ai toujours même coeur; mais je n'ai point de bras" (V.1.1483). From *Nicomède*, "Trois sceptres à son trône attachés par mon bras / Parleront au lieu d'elle, et ne se tairont pas" (I.2.105-06). And from *Horace*, "Aimer un bras souillé du sang de tous mes frères!" (V.3.1619). I myself have tried to dismiss these lines as unfortunate by-products of the rhetorical style. But they would not be dismissed. Gauche, grotesque even, they protrude like obdurate logs amid the flowing alexandrines of Corneille's best plays. To put it less rhetorically, these lines are instances of "marked" language: abnormal, strained discourse which calls attention to its own distortion. Yet extreme as they are, their very extremity makes them emblematic of Corneille's style: by the time we reach *Horace*, his verbal mode has become *foncièrement métonymique*. What is metonymy, and why does it play such a preponderant role in *Horace*? To answer these questions, I will first examine the theoretical foundation of the figure, and then place it within the general thematic and linguistic context of Corneille's play.

Figurative speech is currently receiving a good deal of attention from critics and philosophers. But as Mark Johnson has pointed out, most of this attention has focused on metaphor. In his words, "We are in the midst of a metaphormania" (ix). According to Gérard Genette, this "metaphormania" dates from the early nineteenth century (32). The rhetoricians of that time gave preeminence to metaphor and placed all other figures, including metonymy, in a subordinate position. Today, there is still a tendency to assimilate metonymy to metaphor, as this quote from John R. Searle indicates: "According to my account of metaphor, it becomes a matter of terminology whether we want to construe metonymy and synecdoche as special cases of metaphor or as independent tropes... In each case, as in metaphor proper, the semantic content of the P term conveys the semantic content of the R term by some principle of association. Since the principles of metaphor are rather various anyway, I am inclined to treat metonymy and synecdoche as special cases of metaphor..." (quoted in Johnson 279-80).

However, this reduction of metonymy to metaphor is not wholly satisfying. While both figures substitute one term for another, they do so through opposing linguistic operations. Metaphor expands the verbal field by introducing areas of comparison. Etymologically, it is a "carrying over" of meaning from one semantic zone to another. The definitions of metaphor in both the French Academy and the Furetière dictionaries use the term *transporter*, to carry across. According to the Académie, metaphor is a "Figure de discours qui renferme une espèce de comparaison et par laquelle on transporte un mot de son sens propre et naturel dans un autre sens." And Furetière defines it as a "Figure de rhétorique qui se fait quand un nom propre se transporte d'une chose à une autre qui n'en a point." In *Poetic Diction*, Owen Barfield draws the further inference, already implied by Furetière, that metaphor creates new meanings: "any specifically *new* use of a word or phrase is really a metaphor, since it attempts to arouse cognition of the unknown by suggestion from the known" (112).

Metonymy, on the other hand, is a figure of reduction. The Robert dictionary describes it as a "procédé de langage par lequel on exprime un concept au moyen d'un terme désignant un autre concept qui lui est lié par une relation nécessaire (la cause pour l'effet, le contenant pour le contenu, le signe pour la chose signifiée)." Rather than creating new meanings, metonymy limits meaning to a single, preestablished connection: the sceptre for the kingdom, the arm for the warrior. As we will see, the reductive nature of metonymy makes it particularly congruent to Corneille's vision in *Horace*.

For any Cornelian hero, self-realization implies self-limitation. His heroic characters (that is, those who have an innate penchant for self-assertion) are obliged to choose a set of values and priorities through which their will can manifest itself: in Cornelian terms, *à trancher, à prendre parti*. This moral choice entails the rejection of all conflicting possibilities and desires; even, at times, of a vital part of oneself. Nevertheless, it is an operation they are compelled to perform. Whatever its cost, the hero's identification with a well-defined, narrowly limited, moral perspective is the necessary prelude to heroism. He or she must, as it were, strip for action by eliminating all traces of ambivalence and uncertainty.

The first step in this process is to establish one's position by a conscious act of will. In *Le Cid*, Rodrigue exhorted himself to take up a role. In *Horace*, the characters frequently exhort one another. Horace tells his wife, "Sois plus femme que soeur" (IV.7.1361), and his sister, "Armez-vous de constance, et montrez-vous ma soeur" (II.4.517), while old Horace simply tells his son, "Vis toujours en Horace" (V.3.721). This *prise de position* is accompanied by, and inseparable from, a choice of perspective. As Camille explains to Sabine, where you stand determines what you see: "Parlez plus sainement de vos maux et des miens: / Chacun voit ceux d'autrui d'un autre oeil que les siens" (877-78). As for Camille herself, she has eyes (and ears) only for Curiace: "Tout ce que je voyais me semblait Curiace; / Tout ce qu'on me disait me parlait de ses feux; / Tout ce que je disais l'assurait de mes voeux" (I.2.208-10). It is this single eye, this choice of a unique vision, which empowers the characters to act. Even though Horace must fight against his own kin, his commitment to Rome makes everything simple: "Rome a choisi mon bras, je n'examine rien" (II.3.498). And Camille, preparing to confront Horace, no longer considers herself as a sister, but only as a lover: "préparons-nous à montrer constamment / Ce que doit une amante à la mort d'un amant" (IV.5.1249-50).

This evolution from self-definition to self-fulfillment in action is accomplished through language. For example, Corneille constantly uses verbs of division to indicate the limits imposed on the self: *réduire*, (*se*) *déchirer*, *unir/désunir*, *arracher*, *partager*, *séparer*, *attacher/détacher*, *trancher* and, of course, *diviser*. Indeed, the play abounds in images of division, including the *partage* of the Horaces and Curiaces into threes. Many of the parallel constructions in the play are grouped into fours (*Rome* ... *Rome* ... *Rome* ... *Rome*), and Corneille exploits the convention of calling a spouse a *moitié*: through marriage, the wife literally becomes half of her husband's self (V.3.1606-10).

Once the role is chosen, epithets serve to define and defend one's own stand and to repudiate others'. When Horace praises his own efforts at self-realization, self-denial is termed *sacrifice*; when Camille is attacking this moral stand, sacrifice becomes *barbarisme* or *inhumanité*. Even the same words take on alternately positive and negative meanings: in Sabine's mouth, the epithet *grands coeurs* is savagely ironic (II.6.665). On a syntactic level, antitheses and oppositions combine with epithets to reinforce this effect. Thus, Camille says, "Dégénérons, mon coeur, d'un si vertueux père; / Soyons indigne soeur d'un si généreux frère: / C'est gloire de passer pour un coeur abattu, / Quand la brutalité fait la haute vertu" (IV.4.1239-42).

Both this moral dynamic, and the dramatic language which enacts it, are familiar features of Corneille's work. But there is a basic difference. In *Horace*, unlike *Le Cid*, self-fulfillment is failed or flawed — it either aborts or produces monsters. This is because the choices offered the characters can neither be reduced nor reconciled. What accounts for the radical nature of choice in *Horace*? Critics have often attributed it to moral or psychological factors; but in this particular play, it seems to me that the historical and political constraints are paramount. Corneille is depicting a moment in history when the old system of tribal concord (represented metonymically by *sang*, *noeuds*, *liens*) is being supplanted by the holistic unity of the modern state. Whether or not Corneille is indulging in political anachronism, the "new" regime, as he presents it, replaces traditional family ties by out-and-out assimilation. As the dictator of Albe says, "Nous ne sommes qu'un sang et qu'un peuple en deux villes" (I.2.291). We two are one: a simple ideal to claim, but, as all couples know, not a simple one to achieve or to maintain.

As the political net tightens around the characters, collective union is achieved only through the sacrifice of individual integrity and wholeness. Not surprisingly, certain are unwilling to make this sacrifice. The opposition between totalitarian commitment and individual completeness is conveyed — in a typically Cornelian way — not just by the characters' words but by their very syntax. On the one hand, the Curiace party sees role choice as a matter of proportion. Yes, one role must dominate — *on est plus soeur que femme, ou plus femme que soeur* — but neither duty obliterates the other. The syntax of this groups is marked by structures of relation and comparison: *plus que*, *moins que*, *tant que*, *assez de*, *trop de*, etc. Sabine defines her duty in the following terms:

> Ma constance du moins règne encor sur mes yeux:
> Quand on arrête là les déplaisirs d'une âme,
> Si l'on fait *moins qu'un* homme, on fait *plus qu'une* femme;
> Commander à ses pleurs en cette extrémité,
> C'est montrer pour le sexe *assez de* fermeté. (I.1.10-14)

Julie shows a similar concern with limits and proportion:

> *C'est assez* de constance en un si grand danger
> Que de le voir, l'attendre, et ne point s'affliger;
> Mais certes *c'en est trop* d'aller jusqu'à la joie. (I.1.125-27)

But it is, appropriately, Curiace whose syntax shows the greatest commitment to wholeness and balance:

> J'aime *encor* mon honneur en adorant Camille.
> *Tant qu'*a duré la guerre, on m'a vu constamment
> *Aussi* bon citoyen *que* véritable amant. (I.3.264-66)

If the Curiaces are relativists, the Horaces are absolutists. For them, values can be neither ranked nor quantified. It is not a question of both/and or more/less, but of either/or. Hence, it is fitting that they speak in structures of reduction and exclusion: Curiace's *encore ... en*, *tant que, aussi ... que* give way to *ne ... que*, *ne ... point, tout ou rien*. Instead of *plus ... que*, we have *plus ... plus*. As Camille says to Curiace: "*Plus* ton amour paraît, *plus* elle doit t'aimer; / ... *Plus* tu quittes pour moi, *plus* tu le fais paraître" (I.3.250, 252). Her syntax, like her love, is absolute.

This is not to say that the Horaces completely abandon the rhetoric of comparison. Thus, in I.2, Camille compares her dilemma to Sabine's:

> Croit-elle ma douleur *moins vive que* la sienne
> Et que, *plus* insensible à de si grands malheurs,
> A mes tristes discours je mêle *moins de* pleurs?
> De *pareilles* frayeurs mon âme est alarmée;
> *Comme elle* je perdrai dans l'une et l'autre armée. (136-40)

But her comparison is an arm of combat, lending itself to confrontation rather than compromise. Camille compares in order to defeat.

This combative rhetoric finds its most perfect expression in the exchange between Horace and Curiace prior to their duel (II.3). Curiace first tries to establish a sense of solidarity with Horace in the face of their common predicament:

> Je mets à faire pis, en l'état où nous sommes,
> Le sort, et les démons, et les dieux, et les hommes.
> Ce qu'ils ont de cruel, et d'horrible, et d'affreux,
> L'est bien moins que l'honneur qu'on nous fait *à tous deux*.
> (427-30)

Horace refuses this solidarity. Henceforth, they are intimate enemies who, as the expression goes, can only join in combat: "*S'attacher* au combat *contre un autre soi-même*" (444). Curiace, offended by this rebuff, replies with an ironic reprise of Horce's words: *honneur, vertu, renommée* are projected back and forth as in a *jeu de paume*. Since each character attributes a different meaning to his epithets, no real accord is achieved. In fact, the identity of terms serves to underline the disparity in position. To Horace's "Albe vous a nommé, je ne vous connais plus," Curiace replies, "Je vous connais encore, et c'est ce qui me tue" (502-03). With unconscious prescience, he reveals that his inability to deny an intimate part of himself will be, literally, self-defeating. After this preview, the outcome of the duel is already clear. As Valère reports in IV.2, "En vain en l'attaquant [Curiace] fait paraître un grand coeur, / Le sang qu'il a perdu ralentit sa vigueur" (1117-18). The blood he has lost is also, metonymically, that of his brothers, killed by one who has close ties with his family. In the end, one feels that Curiace is as much weakened by these emotional shocks as by his physical wounds. The dilemma seems complete: by trying to conserve everything he holds important, Curiace loses the most vital thing of all, his life.

Sabine suffers from this dilemma in a different way. Her long monologue in III.1, symmetrically placed at the center of the play, constitutes a rhetorical amplification on the theme of indecision. The monologue itself displays a symmetrical structure, rising to a false climax before falling back into irresolution. Sabine begins by exhorting herself in familiar Cornelian fashion:

> Prenons parti, mon âme, en de telles disgrâces:
> Soyons femme d'Horace, ou soeur des Curiaces;

> Cessons de partager nos inutiles soins;
> Souhaitons quelque chose, et craignons un peu moins. (711-14)

As in the *stances du Cid*, the *-ons* imperative signals an attempt to achieve integrity: to pull oneself (or one's selves) together. But this imperative toward union is placed within linguistic structures of discord: *femme* ou *soeur*, *partager*, *un sort si contraire*, *d'un epoux* ou *d'un frère*. Nevertheless, an attempt at resolution occurs under the aegis of family honor: "Soyons femme de l'un *ensemble et* soeur des autres" (720). Sabine sets out to accomplish this goal by narrowing the verbal and intellectual perspective. This verbal strategy is made explicit in line 725: "*N'appelons point alors* les destins inhumains." The *alors*, here, is instrumental as much as logical: Sabine is trying to change her situation by *calling* things what she wants them to be. The imperatives — *songeons*, *revoyons* — guide her thoughts along proper lines; attribution (*n'appelons*) and reduction (*sans que*, *toute sans*) prevent her from seeing what should not be seen. Language is a channel that narrows and strengthens the heroic conscience.

This movement culminates in a premature cry of triumph: "Fortune, quelques maux que ta rigueur m'envoie, / J'ai trouvé les moyens d'en tirer de la joie" (735-36). These lines are deeply neo-Stoic; momentarily, at least, Sabine finds it possible to change herself, and her fortune, through language. In this very moment of rational *hubris*, her discourse overtops itself. The reductive syntax still dominates; but slowly, ineluctably, unwelcome perceptions begin to seep back under the rhetorical dams designed to hold them. The word *voir* itself changes its meaning: "Et puis *voir* aujourd'hui le combat sans terreur, / Les morts sans désespoir, les vainqueurs sans horreur" (737-38). Perspective shifts from willed to imagined vision as Sabine begins, despite herself, to *see* the victors not without, but with, *horreur*.

This reversal is consecrated in the oxymoron *flatteuse illusion, erreur douce et grossière* (739). Sabine's disillusionment then unfolds in the form, rare for Corneille, of an extended simile, poised motionless at the midpoint of the action:

> Pareille à ces éclairs qui, dans le fort des ombres,
> Poussent un jour qui fuit, et rend les nuits plus sombres,
> Tu n'as frappé mes yeux d'un moment de clarté
> Que pour les abîmer dans plus d'obscurité. (743-46)

The poetic quality of these lines is reinforced by the nominative adjective, *le fort des ombres*, already archaic in Corneille's time. From within this poetic vision, Sabine now rejects her earlier words as a vast rationalization: reason (*vain effort de mon âme*) is no longer a guiding light, but a *faux brillant*.

From this moment on, Sabine redescends into suffering and indecision: "Je sens mon triste coeur percé de tous les coups / Qui m'ôtent *maintenant* un frère ou mon époux" (749-50, emphasis mine). This image, overblown by modern standards, evokes Baroque paintings of martyrdom: St. Sebastian or the Sacred Heart pierced by arrows. In contrast to the more intellectual verbs of will and vision, *je sens* comes from another dimension, that of empathetic sensibility.

This sensibility makes Sabine incapable of maintaining the verbal stance of the Cornelian hero. She is a sheep in wolf 's clothing, essaying a discourse which does not fit her. This incongruity is, in a complete sense, psycho-linguistic. Sabine's speech, like Rodrigue's, aims at the performative: at words doing what they say. When this performative fusion works, Cornelian rhetoric attains its sublime moments. But the language gains rhetorical momentum by sacrificing mimetic power, by cutting its ties to the world. That is why Cornelian characters verge on the maniac, or at least the monomaniac: they see, and say, only what they choose. In Sabine's speech, however, unbidden vision slips in: she *sees* the fraternal dead and, what is worse, the fratricidal victors. More clear-sighted than a true Cornelian heroine, her lucidity will ultimately place her among the vanquished. Nevertheless, Corneille at least accords Sabine, and us, a moment of poetic wholeness amid the metonymic discourse of division. The *faux-brillant* of poetry retains a central place in his creation.

After this moment of connection, Sabine reenters the world of Rome and Alba with its tortured dichotomies:

> Quand je songe à leur mort, quoi que je me propose,
> Je songe par quels bras, et non pour quelle cause,
> Et ne vois les vainqueurs en leur illustre rang
> Que pour considérer aux dépens de quel sang. (751-54)

In larger structural terms, as a careful reader will have noticed, the end of the monologue contains an ironic reprise and reversal of lines taken from its beginning. Thus, line 752 is an inversion of line 726, lines 753-54 reverse the order of 729-30, and so forth. *Alors* (725), marking the preliminary false conclusion, is replaced in ironic echo by *donc*: "C'est là *donc* cette paix que j'ai tant souhaitée!" (759). The monologue impotently ends with an apostrophe to the gods which recalls Curiace's imprecations in II.3. It is no longer possible to triumph over fate, only to accuse it.

Sabine's failure to *prendre parti* affirms her humanity, but deprives her of the power to act or even to influence action. For her, the only solution is to die; but, unlike Camille, she does not even achieve that. Like Chimène in the latter acts of *Le Cid*, she will remain on the sidelines, a pathetic, slightly comic figure of female deploration. For the *plainte*, according to Horace, is a form of discourse fitting only for women, who cannot act in their own right. As he says at the end of II.3, in a final insult to Curiace:

> Et, puisque vous trouvez plus de charme à la plainte,
> En toute liberté goûtez un bien si doux.
> Voici venir ma soeur pour se plaindre avec vous. (508-10)

As events will prove, Horace does an injustice to his sister. Whereas Curiace and Sabine fail to fulfill themselves and to impose their will, Camille and Horace succeed only too well. One might say that, in their case, the ego operation is successful, but both patients expire: Camille literally dying, and Horace suffering an impairment of his heroic identity (*sa gloire ternie*). The Cornelian paradox is complete: while self-limitation permits heroic action, it also reduces individual potential. In other words, the hero becomes self-destructive when he identifies too closely with a single mission — when there is no longer any "play" to his role-playing. Polyeucte's iconoclasm will be tantamount to chopping off his own head; Horace lives on victorious, but only after he has killed all other possibilities within himself.

This radical reduction of the self is conveyed in *Horace* through a trenchant use of metonymy. Appropriately, the most frequent and striking Cornelian metonymies connote mutilation or injury. They usually refer to detached parts of the body — *coeur*, *yeux*, *mains*, *bras* — or to body fluids: *sang*, *larmes*. Further, they are often couched in figures of division — "Son sang dans une armée, et son amour dans l'autre" (I.1.100) — or of reduction; "je n'ai plus d'yeux pour vous" (II.6.590). But these instances of metonymy, while relevant to Corneille's theme, remain within the mainstream of convention. What makes Corneille's metonymic rhetoric unusual is that the mutilation of the person is accompanied by an amplification of the figure. In *Horace*, if I may be permitted to say so, metonymy gets out of hand.

An example may help clarify this point. When Curiace says to Camille in the phrase quoted above, "je n'ai plus d'yeux pour vous"

(II.6.590), we do not take much notice; long before the popular song, this sort of thing was a cliché. But when he repeats the line and continues, "vous en avez pour moi," we are brought up against the *outré* quality of the figure itself. The metonymic process produces a distortion of perspective; like a deforming mirror, it changes the proportions of things.

This distortion of perspective is brought to a head in IV.5, through a central metonymic device of the play, Horace's superhuman arm. Like *main* and *coeur*, *bras* is a kind of abstract synecdoche: the man, Horace, is confined to his destructive instrumentality. But at the same time, the word *bras* itself displays an unsettling tendency to move from the figurative to the corporeal level; it is both metonymically and literally true that the Curiaces are slain by Horace's arm. And in his confrontation with Camille, this ambiguity is pushed to the extreme. When Horace walks on stage brandishing the Curiace swords, the arm becomes the man. "Voici le bras," he states four times, meaning both "I am the arm" and "this is the arm" that liberated Rome. And in the end, this is the arm that will murder his sister. Camille had warned him: "Ne cherche plus ta soeur où tu l'avais laissée; / Tu ne revois en moi qu'une amante offensée, / Qui, comme une furie attachée à tes pas, / Te veut incessamment reprocher son trépas" (IV.5.1283-86). Having chosen her role, Camille acts it out vigorously, hurling epithets at Horace and his beloved Rome until he responds to her verbal attack with the physical aggression she sought.

As this climactic scene reveals, the peculiar intensity of *Horace* arises from its tightness on all stylistic and thematic levels. Camille's punishment is disproportionate to her crime, and the distortion of moral perspective it implies is communicated by the hypertrophy of the figure. If, as one critic has said, Phèdre is an oxymoron personified, then Horace is a walking metonymy. After this scene, *bras* reverts to a more conventional linguistic function, but its metonymic impact remains: in act V, Horace is reduced to an instrument of national destiny, an arm of the state. For the solution proposed by the king is a political one, which claims neither to resolve all problems nor to retrieve all losses. Union is reestablished on the social level, but individual integrity suffers. Unlike Rodrigue, who achieves heroic self-possession in combat and seems to draw vitality from his own conflicts, Horace is defeated even in victory. And as we have seen, the constraints placed on the characters — their *gêne* — is rhetorically imprinted in the language. Without treading the treacherous ground of authorial intent, one can say that *Horace* reveals a consistent and artful pattern of metonymic exacerbation. In both a literal and a figurative sense, the hero is reduced to an extremity. By pushing language and action to the breaking point, Corneille creates that feeling of strangeness within the familiar which constitutes, for many, the essence of art.

In *Horace*, rhetoric becomes reductive in the military sense of the word: the hero is "reduced" as if by siege. *Polyeucte* operates within a similar linguistic system, but the characters will finally recover part of their lost wholeness. In both plays, the audience is first lulled into a false security. In *Horace*, we believe at first that the conflict will be averted and the lovers reunited. And at the beginning of *Polyeucte*, the main character, in his reluctance to leave his new wife to be baptized, appears as perfect a lover as Curiace. In II.4, Polyeucte makes this ardent declaration of love:

> Qu'aux dépens d'un beau feu vous me rendez heureux!
> Et que vous êtes doux à mon coeur amoureux!
> Plus je vois mes défauts et plus je vous contemple,
> Plus j'admire... (623-26)

Nothing seems likely to stand in the way of their marital happiness. This scene is interrupted by the arrival of Cléon, informing Polyeucte that he is expected at the temple. In the course of the next twenty lines, he will be transformed from passionate lover into zealous Christian:

> Allons, mon cher Néarque, allons aux yeux des hommes
> Braver l'idôlatrie, et montrer qui nous sommes. (645-46)

One moment he is reassuring his wife; the next, he is planning to desecrate the temple.

Amid the general controversy surrounding the play, this sudden shift has, from the outset, invited special criticism: is Polyeucte a hypocrite, a liar, or simply demented? In Corneille's defense, Georges Couton argues at length that Polyeucte's behavior falls within the orthodox bounds of sainthood (1638-57). This discussion illustrates some of the interpretive confusions still enveloping Corneille. In one sense, the pious enemies of seventeenth-century theater saw clearly: there *is* a basic difference between theology and theatricality, and Corneille, whatever his personal beliefs, clearly chose the latter over the former. Polyeucte's sudden resolution makes for a wonderful *coup de théâtre*, all the more effective for its unbelievability. As Corneille himself wrote, "Les grands sujets doivent aller au-delà du vraisemblable" (*Premier discours* 2).

The same remark holds good on a psychological level. Certainly, even after his conversion, it is possible to imagine that Polyeucte's feelings for his wife remain unchanged, though overshadowed by stronger feelings. In this light, one can take his rudeness and *gaucherie* as signs of a continuing, involuntary attachment. At the beginning of the play, he is able, like Horace, to overcome his passion by physically removing himself: "Je sens déjà mon coeur prêt à se révolter, / Et ce n'est qu'en fuyant que j'y puis résister" (I.2.123-24). Later, a virtual prisoner of love, he is forced three times to suffer Pauline's visits, without possibility of escape. Finally, he explodes in frustration:

> Après avoir deux fois essayé la menace,
> Après m'avoir fait voir Néarque dans la mort,
> Après avoir tenté l'amour et son effort,
> Après m'avoir montré cette soif du baptême,
> Pour opposer à Dieu l'intérêt de Dieu même,
> Vous vous joignez ensemble! Ah! ruses de l'enfer!
> Faut-il tant de fois vaincre avant que triompher!
> (V.3.1648-54)

The anaphoral *Après* ... *Après* summarizes the action up to this point and carries Polyeucte, on the crest of a rhetorical wave, into his final *Credo* (see below, pp. 50-52).

In a sense, however, the preceding analysis does injustice to Corneille's audacity and originality. Whatever attempts one makes to regularize them, Polyeucte's actions — and even more, his words — remain outrageous. As a result, the spectator's reactions pass from indignation to amazement to bemusement — perhaps a close approximation of the *admiration* Corneille sought to inspire. Two more examples may make this point clear. First, one aspect of *Polyeucte* which came under immediate criticism was the relationship between Pauline and Sévère: many felt that this mixture of gallantry and martyrdom was in doubtful taste, at best. The ingenious critic, however, might find a technical justification for this subplot: that is, Corneille creates the role of Sévère in order to give the play a tragicomic "happy ending." Polyeucte himself lends support to this hypothesis in IV.1, when he says to his guards:

> Mais comme il suffira de trois à me garder,
> L'autre m'obligerait d'aller quérir Sévère;
> Je crois que sans péril on peut me satisfaire:
> Si j'avais pu lui dire un secret important,
> Il vivrait plus heureux, et je mourrais content. (1096-1100)

But as soon as one looks closely at the text, this supposition is exploded. Once again, Corneille's ingenuity exceeds that of his critics. Who would have imagined that upon seeing his wife for the last time, Polyeucte would immediately say to her: "Vivez avec Sévère," compounded by "Vivez avec Sévère, ou mourez avec moi?" (V.3.1584, 1609). These lines, as Pauline's reaction shows, are much worse than the famous "Je ne vous connais plus, si vous n'êtes chrétienne" (1612). For a man who is about to die to hand his wife back to her former lover is to carry self-sacrifice to the point of insult. As Pauline says, "Tigre, assassine-moi du moins sans m'outrager" (1585). This situation recalls another offer no woman could accept, Alceste's involuntarily comic proposal to Eliante in *Le Misanthrope*: "Vengez-moi ... en recevant mon coeur" (IV.2.1249-52). A grimmer smile is provoked by Polyeucte's injunction to Félix, which also has Moliéresque tonalities:

> Non, non, persécutez,
> Et soyez l'instrument de nos félicités:
> Celle d'un vrai chrétien n'est que dans les souffrances;
> Les plus cruels tourments lui sont des récompenses. (V.2.1533-36)

This may be tragicomedy, but not of the received kind. As in *L'Illusion*, *Le Cid*, and even *Horace*, Corneille's pursuit of rhetorical extremity takes him back and forth across the boundary separating comedy from tragedy. For Polyeucte, like Horace, is an absolutist. I use the word advisedly: while no powerful sovereign appears in *Polyeucte*, the play is imbued with an absolutist vision which fuses together all political, religious and personal elements. On the linguistic level, *souverain*, *absolu* and equivalent terms appear frequently. *Souverain*, like its etymological double *suprême*, comes from the Latin *superamus*, "highest." Its secondary, political meanings, which later become dominant, are derived from this primary sense. In *Polyeucte*, these epithets retain much of their original meaning: to worship the sovereign is to identify with the highest good. Thus, Sévère says in II.1:

> Pourrai-je voir Pauline, et rendre à ses beaux yeux
> L'hommage *souverain* que l'on va rendre aux dieux? (367-68)

For Sévère, in keeping with the courtly tradition, love exercises supreme authority over the lover, preempting both political and religious obligations. Pauline uses the word in a similar sense: "Tant qu'ils ne sont qu'amants nous sommes *souveraines*" (I.3.133).

In these examples, the word has already taken on the metaphorical sense defined by Littré: "Il se dit de l'empire que l'on a sur ses passions, sur son âme, sur le coeur d'un autre." Littré gives an example from *Polyeucte*: "Et sur mes passions ma raison *souveraine* / Eût blâmé mes soupirs et dissipé ma haine" (II.2.477-78).

To this example, one could add the following:

> Ainsi de vos désirs toujours *reine absolue* (II.2.481)

> Ma raison, il est vrai, dompte mes sentiments;
> Mais quelque autorité que sur eux elle ait prise,
> Elle n'y règne pas, elle les tyrannise; (500-02)

Love (dominion over the love-object) and self-control (dominion over one's own feelings) are seen as parallel phenomena, both part of the *empire des passions*.

For Pauline and Sévère, who are primarily concerned with their private lives and feelings, it is not surprising that the *souverain empire* is psychological. For Polyeucte, sovereignty lies in a different realm. He says of baptism:

> Bien que je le préfère aux grandeurs d'un empire,
> Comme le bien *suprême* et le seul où j'aspire,
> Je crois pour satisfaire un juste et saint amour,
> Pouvoir un peu remettre, et différer d'un jour. (I.1.49-52)

As the clauses of concession show, Polyeucte is not yet an absolutist. Yes, baptism is the supreme good, but it is paramount in a hierarchical structure which reserves space for other obligations. Furetière's dictionary illustrates this hierarchical concept of sovereignty both explicitly, through definition, and implicitly, through the very order of the entries:

> (1) Le premier Etre, le Tout-Puissant. ...
> (2) à l'égard des hommes, se dit des rois, des Princes qui n'ont Personne au dessus d'eux qui leur commande, qui ne relevent que de Dieu & de leur épée.
> (3) se dit aussi des Juges qui ont pouvoir du roi ...

Furetière does not extend the notion of sovereignty down into private life, but classical usage clearly does.

Néarque's reply, while more extremist, still maintains this hierarchical view:

> Nous pouvons tout aimer, il le souffre, il l'ordonne;
> Mais, à vous dire tout, ce Seigneur des seigneurs
> Veut le premier amour et les premiers honneurs.
> Comme rien n'est égal à sa grandeur *suprême*,
> Il faut ne rien aimer qu'après lui, qu'en lui-même,
> Négliger, pour lui plaire, et femme, et biens, et rang,
> Exposer pour sa gloire et verser tout son sang. (70-76)

This speech displays an interesting ambivalence. The first part, with its noble vocabulary (*seigneur*, *grandeur*) evokes the image of a feudal monarchy in which the ruler is supreme but not absolute. The last three lines, however, move from a multivalent, hierarchical system to a unitary, absolutist one: *après lui* is supplanted by *en lui-même*, which is then reinforced by *négliger ... verser tout son sang*. For Néarque, Christianity's sovereignty is not yet total: one neglects other loves, but does not abandon them. As Polyeucte's destiny unfolds, he will take this further, radical step.

Polyeucte's shift from limited to absolute sovereignty is developed in three passages which outline the tenets of the Christian faith. These share as subtext the Credo of the Latin mass, universally familiar to French audiences from Corneille's time well into the twentieth century:

> Credo in unum Deum, Patrem omnipotentem, factorem caeli et terrae, visibilium omnium et invisibilium. Et in unum Dominum Iesum Christum, Filium Dei unigenitum. ...

A comparison between the liturgical and the Cornelian texts reveals basic shifts in emphasis. In the first passage, Stratonice recounts Polyeucte's desecration of the temple and reports his words:

> Le Dieu de Polyeucte et celui de Néarque
> De la terre et du ciel est l'absolu monarque,
> Seul être indépendant, seul maître du destin,
> Seul principe éternel, et souveraine fin.
> C'est ce Dieu des chrétiens qu'il faut qu'on remercie
> Des victoires qu'il donne à l'empereur Décie;
> Lui seul tient en sa main le succès des combats;
> Il le veut élever, il le peut mettre à bas;
> Sa bonté, son pouvoir, sa justice est immense. (III.2.841-49)

Certain of Stratonice's terms, like *bonté*, *pouvoir*, *justice* are biblical and liturgical, but others, like *l'absolu monarque* and *maître du destin*, apply more aptly to a political ruler than a divine one.

This tendency toward politicization continues into the second passage (IV.6), where Sévère comments, as an impartial observer, on the characteristics of Christianity. Like Polyeucte (as quoted by Stratonice), Sévère offers a gloss on the first line of the Credo (*Credo in unum Deum, patrem omnipotentem / Les chrétiens n'ont qu'un Dieu, maître absolu de tout*); and like Polyeucte's, his version changes the paternal to the monarchical (*patrem omnipotentem* > *maître absolu*). He also asserts that the strength of Christianity lies in its monotheistic premise: one absolute God ruling the universe, as opposed to a mob of weak and warring deities. Finally, Sévère places a greater emphasis on divine will than one finds in the liturgical text: "De qui le seul vouloir fait tout ce qu'il résout" (1430). Thus, the language of these two preliminary credos creates a monarchical image of God, in which the divine becomes a representation of the royal, rather than the (expected) reverse.

These tendencies come to full fruition in Polyeucte's *credo* which, not incidentally, also marks the dramatic high point of the play — a real "show-stopper." At last, Polyeucte speaks in his own voice about the attributes of God and his own relation to Him. Polyeucte's speech reiterates the changes we already found in the earlier passages (emphasis on monotheism, secular *maîtrise* of God, etc.), while heightening the emotional intensity of the text. The Credo is not, on the whole, one of the more dramatic parts of the Mass; setting this prolonged catalogue of beliefs to music has always posed something of a challenge to composers. Corneille increases the dramatic impact of the passage by subtle syntaxic and lexical changes. While the Latin text begins *Credo in unum Deum* (standard French version "je crois en un seul Dieu"), Polyeucte cries in typical Cornelian fashion: "Je n'adore qu'un Dieu," a more emphatically monotheistic statement than one finds in either the Latin or the modern French versions. Further, he substitutes *adorer* for *croire*. The verb *adorare* does appear later in the Latin text, in the passive construction *Qui cum Patre et Filio simul adoratur* (standard French translation "il reçoit même adoration"). In the context of the Mass, "to adore" is synonym of "to worship"; but in Corneille's context, it leads up to expressions like "Un Dieu qui, nous aimant d'une amour infinie" and "cet excès d'amour" (V.3.1659, 1661) which have no counterpart in the original Credo. Polyeucte portrays

God's love as excessive and, in deciding to sacrifice himself, Polyeucte carries human excess to a transcendent level.

As has often been remarked, the most thrilling (*sublime*) moment of the scene comes with the repeated affirmation, "je suis chrétien." This statement shows a great deal of courage, but no hint of Christian abnegation. By uniting with God, Polyeucte is not diminishing but aggrandizing himself to become all-powerful, independent, self-sustaining — the divinized image, in fact, of the Cornelian hero "de qui le seul vouloir fait tout ce qu'il résout." At this moment, the audience enjoys a kind of vicarious "power trip"; we share in Polyeucte's excitement as he gleefully connects himself to the source of cosmic potency.

Thus, an examination of *Polyeucte* reveals a pervasive politicization extending into all aspects of the play. By gradual linguistic accretions, Corneille transforms the spiritual God of the Credo into an absolute monarch, *un portrait du roi*. The power relations among king and hero are represented in the diagram presented in figure 5. Whether on the individual, the political or the religious level, division leads to weakness. On the individual plane this weakness is evidenced in Felix's collection of unruly and contradictory thoughts:

> De pensers sur pensers mon âme est agitée,
> De soucis sur soucis elle est inquiétée:
> Je sens l'amour, la haine, et la crainte, et l'espoir,
> La joie et la douleur tour à tour l'émouvoir;
> J'entre en des sentiments qui ne sont pas croyables;
> J'en ai de violents, j'en ai de pitoyables;
> J'en ai de généreux qui n'oseraient agir;
> J'en ai même de bas, et qui me font rougir. (III.5.1005-12)

In the political sphere as well, authority is severely fragmented. Félix, the Emperor's representative, is a weak power broker who, as we have seen, fears Polyeucte, Sévère, the gods, and his own shadow. Polyeucte, descendant of local kings, poses a political and religious threat to imperial rule. Sévère, the victorious Roman hero, might decide to reign in his own right. This dispersion of power creates a vacuum which will be filled by the dynamic new force of Christianity. The old gods show the same division as the old men of the Empire. Even Sévère comments on the disaccord among the pagan deities: "Les nôtres bien souvent s'accordent mal ensemble; ... Nous en avons beaucoup pour être de vrais dieux" (IV.6.1432, 1434). This division is carried to its extreme point in Polyeucte's act of iconoclasm:

Levels of Action	*Weakness*	*Strength*
Religious (God)	Polytheism: weak and fragmented divinity (broken idols)	Monotheism: one powerful deity
Political (King)	Political division	Political unity and absolutism
Individual (Hero)	Psychological and moral weakness, indecisiveness, corruption	Moral strength, integrity

Figure 5

he literally reduces the gods to bits and pieces. According to Stratonice's account, first the wine and incense jars are knocked to the ground, then "Du plus puissant des dieux nous voyons la statue / Par une main impie à leurs pieds abattue" (III.2.857-58). And Polyeucte himself vows to build an altar to his God upon a mound of broken idols: "Dressons-lui des autels *sur des monceaux d'idoles*" (II.6.685).

In contrast to the divisive polytheists, Polyeucte is wholly a Christian: "Je suis chrétien, Néarque, et le suis tout à fait"; the effect of baptism acts within him "tout entière" (II.6.667, 695). This wholeness makes itself fully felt after Polyeucte's death, as Pauline and Félix are united through conversion: "Son amour épandu sur toute la famille / Tire après lui le père aussi bien que la fille" (V.6.1775-76). Sévère, though remaining unconverted, pledges an end to the Christian persecutions: "Je perdrai mon crédit envers sa majesté, / Ou vous verrez finir cette sévérité" (1805-06). And Félix's closing lines prefigure a union of religion and *imperium* as he says to Sévère, "Daigne le ciel en vous achever son ouvrage" (1808). We have a happy ending, if not the one expected; Polyeucte's disappearance seems to reconcile everyone and everything. But our analysis has taken a final, curious twist. With a kind of circular reflexivity, both God and monarch become representations of the hero, or, more precisely, of the autonomous (sovereign) will. And Polyeucte's heroic monotheism reveals itself as a form of narcissism, even to the tautological form of the enunciation, *je suis chrétien*. Whether the classical sign, as Jay Caplan suggests, "necessarily acts out an eucharistic scenario" (811), it does have a doubly absolute meaning here: *je suis chrétien* = *je suis moi* = *je suis Dieu*. But this transcendent absolute, in turn, is revealed as a projection of the individual's yearning for absoluteness. *Portrait du roi, portrait du moi*: Polyeucte's *credo* is a tribute to the sovereign ego, his kingdom, the dominion of the self.

Corneille's rhetorical vision comes to a climax with *Nicomède*. As well as echoing earlier plays linguistically, this work resolves thematic problems they have raised. In his comments on *L'Illusion*, Robert Garapon says of Matamore: "On dirait en effet que Corneille, en concevant son héros, a voulu traiter, sur le mode comique, la question générale suivante: dans quelle mesure les paroles peuvent-elles remplacer les actes, ou, si l'on préfère, comment peut-on renverser la maxime latine traditionnelle, et dire désormais: 'verba, non acta'?" (160). Revising this observation, one could say that in *Nicomède*, Corneille treats the same problem in a heroic mode. The question is the following: how can the hero remain a hero when he is prevented by circumstances from performing deeds of valor? Drawn into a trap by his step-mother, isolated from his army, Nicomède finds himself at the mercy of his enemies. In this dilemma, all that is left to him is speech. He keeps Laodice's love, and the people's esteem, through an unrelenting rhetoric of glory. In this effort, it is no wonder that he sometimes sounds like Matamore himself. Short on present deeds, he promises military exploits to come, claiming to Arsinoé:

> Votre amour maternel veut voir régner mon frère;
> Et je contribuerai moi-même à ce dessein,
> Si vous pouvez souffrir qu'il soit roi de ma main.
> Oui, l'Asie à mon bras offre encor des conquêtes;
> Et pour l'en couronner mes mains sont toutes prêtes.
> Commandez seulement, choisissez en quels lieux;
> Et j'en apporterai la couronne à vos yeux. (V.9.1800-06)

Similarly, Matamore had said to Isabelle:

> Choisissez en quels lieux il vous plaît de régner;
> Ce bras tout aussitôt vous conquête un empire:
> J'en jure par lui-même, et cela c'est tout dire. (II.4.416-18)

Isabelle's response will be paraphrased by Arsinoé at the end of *Nicomède*:

> Ne prodiguez pas tant ce bras toujours vainqueur;
> Je ne veux point régner que dessus votre coeur.
> (*L'Illusion* II.4.419-20)
>
> La haute ambition d'un si puissant vainqueur
> Veuille encor triompher jusque dedans mon coeur?
> (*Nicomède* V.9.1809-10)

More subtly, to proclaim his heroism, Nicomède uses the same technique of accumulation that Matamore employed to a comic effect:

> [Grâce] de quoi, madame? Est-ce d'avoir conquis
> Trois sceptres, que ma perte expose à votre fils?
> D'avoir porté si loin vos armes dans l'Asie,
> Que même votre Rome en a pris jalousie?
> D'avoir trop soutenu la majesté des rois?
> Trop rempli votre cour du bruit de mes exploits?
> Trop du grand Annibal pratiqué les maximes?
> S'il faut grâce pour moi, choisissez de mes crimes.
> (IV.2.1153-60)

And Matamore:

> Le seul bruit de mon nom renverse les murailles,
> Défait les escadrons, et gagne les batailles.
> Mon courage invaincu contre les empereurs
> N'arme que la moitié de ses moindres fureurs;
> D'un seul commandement que je fais aux trois Parques,
> Je dépeuple l'Etat des plus heureux monarques;
> Le foudre est mon canon, les Destins mes soldats:
> Je couche d'un revers mille ennemis à bas. (II.2.233-40)

There are obvious differences between the two speeches — Nicomède's is tempered by irony, and Matamore's escapes into mythological fantasy — but both are in the hyperbolic mode, both display the rhetorical "hype" of the self-advertising hero. *Nicomède* also shows a linguistic affinity with *Horace*, through a resurgence of metonymic terms like *bras*, *main*, *coeur*, *nom*, *couronne*, *sceptre*. But while in *Horace*, metonymy was a trope of reduction, here it is a means of compensation or substitution. Laodice had said to Nicomède:

> Et vous flattez point ni sur votre grand coeur,
> Ni sur l'éclat d'un nom cent et cent fois vainqueur;
> Quelque haute valeur que puisse être la vôtre,
> Vous n'avez en ces lieux que deux bras comme un autre.
> (I.1.89-92)

The phrase "deux bras comme un autre" refers back to her evocation of the army as "cent mille bras tout prêts à me venger" (86). But the hero's one rhetorical arm is worth more than two of an ordinary man's. Through metonymy, he projects the power he cannot actualize at the moment. Nicomède himself is well aware of the potency of his words. When Prusias asks him, "Contre elle, dans ma cour, que peut votre insolence?" He replies: "Rien du tout, que garder ou rompre le silence" (II.3.723-24).

Not only does Nicomède's language sustain his status and power; it also serves to guarantee his heroic identity against the pressures of time and change. One of the challenges of the Cornelian hero is to maintain constancy in an inconstant world, ruled by flux and change. In *Le Cid*, this inconstancy is represented by the Moors who literally rise and fall with the tide. According to Rodrigue's poetic account:

> Cette obscure clarté qui tombe des étoiles
> Enfin avec le flux nous fait voir trente voiles;
> L'onde s'enfle dessous, et d'un commun effort
> Les Maures et la mer montent jusques au port...

But in defeat, "Pour souffrir ce devoir leur frayeur est trop forte; / Le flux les apporta, le reflux les remporte" (IV.3.1273-76, 1317-18). The Moors form part of the natural realm; the hero rises above nature by subduing it in himself and in others.

It is one thing to achieve heroism, another to sustain it against the erosion of time. In *L'Illusion*, Dorante and Matamore temporarily escape from reality and duration by an autonomous verbal universe; Rodrique escapes into History by becoming Le Cid. But Don Diège or Horace do not possess an entire heroic existence: "O cruel souvenir de ma gloire passée! / Oeuvre de tant de jours en un jour effacée!" (*Le Cid*: Don Diègue, I.4.245-46). And Horace's situation is worse than Don Diègue's; Rodrigue can save his father's reputation, but Horace sees no way to preserve his own glory. For this reason, he would have preferred to die while it was at its height:

> La mort seule aujourd'hui peut conserver ma gloire:
> Encor la fallait-il sitôt que j'eus vaincu,
> Puisque pour mon honneur j'ai déjà trop vécu.
> (V.2.1580-82)

This problem is resolved in a unique way in *Nicomède*. For the duration of the play, all tensions between drama and rhetoric, plot and speech, disappear, as words take the place of acts. This solution is made possible by the peculiarly contradictory qualities of Nicomède himself, a true, if temporarily impotent, hero. Whereas in *L'Illusion*, Matamore's verbal fantasy was totally unsupported by reality, Nicomède's speech rests on a substrate of real deeds — the heroic coin of the realm. He has won "real" battles, he will win them again; so for the time being, he can keep his momentum going through purely verbal acts. After *Nicomède*, words and things will never again achieve the same balance and congruence. Under the pressures of classical esthetics, Corneille will move away from the free-wheeling rhetorical mode which was spontaneously his. Even the author himself failed to understand, or could not admit, that his characters were true not to some fixed notion of behavior, but to a verbal context.

This movement was a gradual one. In "L'Excuse à Ariste," which preceded and helped provoke the *Querelle du Cid*, Corneille made absolute claims of autonomy and freedom of expression. But the *Querelle* undermined his self-confidence and increased his susceptibility to criticism. According to Chapelain: "Scudéry a du moins gagné cela, en le querellant, qu'il l'a rebuté du métier et lui a tari sa veine ... il ne parle plus que de règles et que de choses qu'il eût pu répondre aux académiciens ..." (Couton 1135). Corneille even went so far as to ask the academician's advice on *Horace* before its presentation, but fortunately did not take it (Couton 1536-37). On the other hand, his preoccupation with the exigencies of plot, in both theory and practice, became more and more marked. *L'Illusion* is a case in point. In the dedicatory letter prefacing the early editions, Corneille describes his creation with pride:

> Voici un étrange monstre que je vous dédie. Le premier acte n'est qu'un Prologue; les trois suivants font une Comédie imparfaite, le dernier est une Tragédie; et tout cela, cousu ensemble, fait une Comédie. Qu'on en nomme l'invention bijarre et extravagante tant qu'on voudra, elle est nouvelle. (613)

In the *Examen* of 1660, however, he speaks of his play's structure with disparagement, almost with embarrassment:

> Je dirai peu de chose de cette Pièce; c'est une galanterie extravagante qui a tant d'irrégularités qu'elle ne vaut pas la peine de la considérer, bien que la nouveauté de ce caprice en ait rendu le succès assez favorable pour ne me repentir pas d'y avoir perdu quelque temps. Le premier Acte ne semble qu'un Prologue; les trois suivants forment une Pièce que je ne sais comment nommer: le succès en est tragique....

While the content of the description has changed relatively little, its tone has altered from admiration to denigration. Corneille continues:

> Tout cela cousu ensemble fait une comédie dont l'action n'a pour durée que celle de sa représentation, mais sur quoi il ne serait pas sûr de prendre exemple. Les caprices de cette nature ne se hasardent qu'une fois; et quand l'original aurait passé pour merveilleux, la copie n'en peut jamais rien valoir. (615)

Corneille clearly maintains a sneaking fondness for his "bijarre" invention, but is not about to repeat it; his own assimilation of classical standards is too complete.

While losing some of their "irregularities," Corneille's later plots display a progressive stylization and rigidity, an almost gratuitous cultivation of parallels and reversals. Already in *Horace*, family relationships resemble a problem in mechanics. When we arrive at *Rodogune*, the imperatives of plot totally supersede other criteria. Critics have wondered why Rodogune, the virtuous heroine, asks the crown princes to kill their mother in III.4. The answer is that in II.3, Cléopâtre had already asked her sons to kill Rodogune, and Corneille wants to compose two symmetrical acts. This concern with the mechanics of plot, to the detriment of psychological plausibility, moves Corneille's play from the domain of drama into that of melodrama.

Thus, the discussion of rhetorical discourse inevitably leads to the larger question of genre. We have already observed in Corneille's plays a constant crossing and recrossing of genre boundaries. In *L'Illusion*, this crossing is conscious and virtuosic; Corneille takes pleasure in playing with, constructing and deconstructing, dramatic forms. Some of the same playfulness is to be observed in *Le Cid*, as the tone shifts from comic to tragi-comic to tragic. Corneille's successive relabelings of the play — *Comédie, Tragicomédie, Tragédie, Tragédie Heureuse* — reflect these variations, as well as the evolution of classical dramatic theory. Even in *Horace*, Corneille manipulates audience expectations with familiar comic techniques like reversal, false death announcements, and misinterpreted messages. But other factors also bring their influence to bear. I would argue that in Corneille's work, genre distinctions result from an interplay of dramatic form, language and values. In *Le Cid*, a basic moral accord gives the characters license to indulge in the free-wheeling rhetoric which Kenneth Burke calls "the dancing of an attitude" (Burke 9). The result is Cornelian comedy, whatever its official label. In *Horace*, where basic values remain irreconcilable and irreducible, characters are trapped in linguistic patterns which lead to dissolution and tragedy. *Polyeucte* offers a way out of this dilemma. While the values of the various characters appear irreconcilable, one value is finally revealed as supreme. By cleaving to this sovereign value, *Polyeucte* both preserves the integrity of the heroic self and recreates the social union. With its final conversions, the play deserves the label of *tragédie heureuse*. In *Nicomède*, as in *Le Cid*, one basic moral vision dominates. Again, dramatic conflict is played out through language, but this conflict, instead of emerging as comedy, is transmuted into irony; everyone recognizes the truth of Nicomède's nobility except the villains, who are dupes of their own fears. Thus, *Nicomède* presents Cornelian *drama* in its purest form; a verbal confrontation that is neither comic nor tragic. Cornelian drama only turns to tragedy when opposing moral perspectives, retaining their legitimacy, tear the characters apart.

Corneille's drama cuts across both neoclassical categories and modern conceptions of a "tragic vision." For purposes of contrast, I will quote from Leo Spitzer's remarks on *Phèdre*. Spitzer's analysis also focuses on language, but to very different ends: "It is highly significant that, in the interpolations of Dämpfung [muting, attenuation], the classical poets put references to that stable world of moral values toward which they most insistently strove" ("Récit de Théramène" 114-15). The striving toward moral values which Spitzer discerns in *Phèdre* is characteristic of Racinian tragedy, but not of Cornelian drama. In tragedy as we most commonly understand it, characters proceed through ignorance to a recognition of truths about human nature and the universal order. Corneille turns things around. Moral and psychological truths are the preconditions of the heroic quest, not its object: the moral code supplies the ground rules according to which the dramatic game will be played.

This interpretation is not designed to discount earlier studies of Cornelian psychology and *morale*. Moral and psychological considerations certainly mattered to Corneille, and his plays would be shallow indeed without them. But one must be careful not to give fictional characters a solidity and three-dimensionality they cannot possess. Serge Doubrovsky talks of the existential nature of the Cornelian hero, his becoming through acts. But more than through acts, the hero becomes through words; his very existence is a verbal vector, propelled by energy and volition. As befits an actor, his central being is performative: Auguste, in *Cinna*, is *maître de soi comme de l'univers* because he *says* so. In the same way, Corneille is a master of the theater because he says so. As Scudéry remarks in his observations on *Le Cid*, and as I have stated less polemically, Corneille's characters always sound alike (Couton 789). That is because their author is always speaking: the actors' performance remains inviolably his. Corneille urges Foucault in the prefatory epistle to *Oedipe*:

> Choisis-moi seulement quelque nom dans l'histoire
> Pour qui tu veuilles place au temple de la Gloire,
> Quelque nom favori qu'il te plaise arracher
> A la nuit de la tombe, aux cendres du bûcher.
> Soit qu'il faille ternir ceux d'Enée et Virgile,
> Par un noble attentat sur Homère et Achille,
> Soit qu'il faille obscurcir par un dernier effort
> Ceux que j'ai sur la scène affranchis de la mort:
> Tu me verras le même....(*Oeuvres*, Seuil II.566)

After more than twenty years of writing, it is difficult to distinguish Corneille's rhetoric from Rodrigue's — or Matamore's.

This identification with his characters defines Corneille's greatness as well as his limits. Even in his best plays, there is a tendency for the characters to be taken over by the author, to become marionettes performing a formal dance on stage. But when it works, Corneille's all-encompassing rhetoric can attain that theatrical power and magic to which even his critics had to pay homage:

> Mais vous dites, Monsieur, qu'il a ébloui les yeux du monde, vous l'accusez de charme et d'enchantement: Je connais beaucoup de gens qui feraient vanité d'une telle accusation; et vous me confesserez vous-même que si la magie était une chose permise, ce serait une chose excellente. (Balzac, quoted in Couton 1465)

3. Racine: Words in Search of Truth

Et ne devrait-on pas à des signes certains
Reconnaître le coeur des perfides humains?
Phèdre IV.1

In the last thirty years the works of Racine have attracted an almost endless variety of "approaches." It is almost as if the critics, perplexed by the deceptive transparency of Racine's poetry, have rushed to fill a void, not in the texts, but in themselves: to "explain" Racine psychologically, sociologically, semiotically, philosophically or, most recently, ideologically.[1] Critics such as Timothy Reiss and Jean-Marie Apostolidès have assigned tragedy a central role within the classical ideology of representation. According to Reiss, tragedy participates in a network of discourses (both scientific and nonscientific) which mesh together to create the "reality" of the classical episteme. With some obvious and necessary differences, he sees the development of classical tragedy as analogous to that of the experimental sciences. The culmination of this development is manifest in the plays of Racine, where "the character becomes a person endowed with psychological depth, and tragedy is taken as a container of certain knowledge showing the moral, psychological and so forth functioning of the individual and society" (*Truth and Tragedy* 5). Reiss expresses his fundamental thesis in the dense formula, a play is a "thought experiment" (219). This Einsteinian phrase implies that a work of literature shares the same epistemological status as a scientific treatise.

[1] Cf., for example, Charles Mauron, *L'Inconscient dans l'oeuvre et la vie de Racine* (Geneva: Slatkine, 1986); Maurice Delacroix, "La Tragédie de Racine est-elle psychologique?" in *Racine: Mythes et réalités*, ed. Constant Venesoen (Paris: Société d'Etude

However, Racine's tragedies have also been read in the opposite direction. Instead of the "container of certain knowledge" perceived by Reiss, Richard Barnett sees an enigmatic world where "there is no certitude, no verifiability" (Barnett 118), where vision is not transparent but blind. Words are, indeed, signs of the hidden, but for that very reason it is impossible to know *what* they hide, or how to make a reliable connection between sign and hidden truth. What relation does Racine's esthetic really bear to the philosophic undercurrents of his time? Does his tragedy share the oft-proclaimed certainties of classical philosophy or its shadowy doubts? In poetic terms, is Racine's discourse of light or of darkness?

There are two ways to approach this question: through Racine's writing about literature and through his own literary works. Like other great (or even not-so-great) writers, Racine was also a great reader. He distinguished himself from his contemporaries by a deep knowledge of, and sensitivity to, the Greek poets, many of whom he studied and annotated in detail. Yet, according to Raymond Picard, those who turn to Racine's commentaries on Greek authors for a key to the French poet's own vision will be sorely disappointed:

> Seul devant Sophocle, et loin d'un public importun, Racine n'allait-il pas enfin se laisser aller à des confidences sur son art? Hélas, il faut bien en convenir: tout ce que Racine avait à dire à Sophocle, à Euripide, ou presque tout, il l'a exprimé — et non sans bonheur, reconnaissons-le — dans *Iphigénie* ou dans *Phèdre*. (Picard II.649-50)

I would differ with Picard's assertion. Particularly in his remarks on the *Odyssey*, Racine, from a poet's point of view, touches on the problem of representation. He quotes, for example, the following passage from the *Odyssey* describing Ulysses' visit to the Phaecians:

> Et tous, près de leur père et de leur digne mère, vivent à banqueter; leurs tables sont chargées de douceurs innombrables; tout le jour, la maison, dans le fumet des graisses, retentit de leurs voix; la nuit, chacun s'en va, près de sa chaste épouse, dormir sur le tapis de son cadre ajouré. (X.8-12)

du XVIIe, 1976); Lucien Goldmann, *Le Dieu caché* (Paris: Gallimard, 1967); Danielle Kaisergruber et al. *Phèdre de Racine: pour une sémiotique de la représentation classique* (Paris: Larousse, 1972); Louis Marin, *Portrait du roi* (Paris: Minuit, 1981); Jean-Marie Apostolidès, *Le Prince sacrifié* (Paris: Minuit, 1985); and a general article with the significant title, "Racine en proie à la critique moderne," by Françoise Reiss, *Cahiers Raciniens* 29 (1971) 13-62.

Racine comments on this passage: "Cela représente parfaitement bien une maison paisible et commode, et qui n'est troublée d'aucune division" (Picard II.797).[2] This comment indicates that representation, for Racine, means more than a simple reflection of the world. Certainly, he is attracted by Homer's precision, his references to authentic wines drunk in ancient Greece, to actual herbs described by Pliny, by all the rich realism which the *délicatesse* of French conventions will not allow (Picard II.804). The phrase "fumet des graisses," for example, would never appear in a French epic poem of Racine's time. But his interests go beyond physical description to the conveying by concrete means of an abstract psychological or moral truth. Thus, in the quotation above, tastes, sounds and smells all contribute to an impression of domestic harmony.

This search for an abstract meaning behind the concrete also manifests itself in Racine's choice of verbs. For example, he comments on Ulysses' speech in V.222-24: "On *voit* là un beau caractère, d'un esprit fort et résolu, qui ne craint point les traverses." Racine also observes that Homer says something in order to show (*montrer*) something else (Picard II.749, 757, 759). Finally, and perhaps most significantly, he uses the word *marque*: "c'est une marque d'un esprit bien né" (768): "discours d'Achille, qui marque sa fierté" (713). Thus, in Racine's reading of Homer, representation places itself within an abstract order where both words and things are psychological signs (*marques*).

Thus, despite his ocular vocabulary, Racine's vision, as Richard Barnett has pointed out, is not a simple form of sight: "In Racine's tragedy, 'visual' terminologies... do not function on a wholly mimetic plane, and certainly not on any level of literality" (Barnett 116). This intertwining of the thought and the perceived is at the heart of classical representation. According to Littré, the primary sense of the term "representation" is "visual" — "se présenter devant les yeux." The second and third definitions also emphasize the role of sight: "en être l'image" and "figurer." But in the latter cases, ocular representation simultaneously involves a mental act of imagination or cognition. This concept makes it necessary to clarify the relations of the image to the "inner space" of the mind, on the one hand, and the outside world on the other. These are the relations which Racine develops in his

[2] Quotations from Racine are taken from the Picard edition in two volumes (see list of works cited). Since the lines in the plays are not numbered, references are to page numbers, unless otherwise indicated.

plays, and which I will begin to examine under the *chiaroscuro* illumination of *Andromaque*.

Andromaque is often read as a tragedy of individual passion. In the traditional *boutade*, Oreste loves Hermione who loves Pyrrhus who loves Andromaque who loves a dead man. According to Martin Turnell, this amorous chain unchains the disaster. "Once the paroxysm has begun, nothing can stop it... For moderation in any form is impossible and abhorrent; the suggestion that they should even listen to reason is felt to be an intolerable affront..." (*The Classical Moment* 176). Without dismissing the role of psychological causality, it must be examined within a literary and esthetic context. After all, and above all, Racine was not a psychologist but a *writer*; and his writing, in *Andromaque*, turns on an image. I refer, of course, to the vision of Troy, which Andromaque, Pyrrhus and the others irrevocably carry before their eyes. As Racine states in his preface, he has changed the plot of Euripedes' tragedy to emphasize this linkage with Troy:

> Andromaque ne connaît point d'autre mari qu'Hector, ni d'autre fils qu'Astyanax. J'ai cru en cela me conformer à l'idée que nous avons maintenant de cette princesse. La plupart de ceux qui ont entendu parler d'Andromaque ne la connaissent guère que pour la veuve d'Hector et pour la mère d'Astyanax. (IV.243)

Yet Euripides' version, despite the substitution of Pyrrhus' son for Hector's, also portrays Andromaque as a vestige of a devastated past, an exile fallen from glory. Both Euripides' and Racine's visions are drawn from Virgil, in particular the elegiac evocations of Book III of the *Aeneid*. This tone is captured in the Pléiade translation:

> Lorsqu'il eut paru bon à ceux d'En Haut, contre toute justice, de renverser l'empire d'Asie et la nation de Priam, et que la superbe Ilion fut tombée, et que tout ce qui avait été Troie bâtie par Neptune ne fut plus qu'un sol fumant, les signes que nous donnèrent les dieux nous poussèrent à chercher de lointains exils dans un monde désert. (1-6)

As we will see, this vision will also nourish, in a different context, Racine's biblical drama: the destruction of Jerusalem and the Babylonian exile in *Esther*. In *Andromaque*, Racine's poetics of destruction juxtaposes what remains (*reste*) with what is lost (*perte*). Pyrrhus' description of Troy contains both these elements, and recalls Virgil's depiction of the ravaged city, quoted above:

> ... et je regarde enfin
> Quel fut le sort de Troie, et quel est son destin:
> Je ne vois que des tours que le cendre a couvertes,
> Un fleuve teint de sang, des campagnes désertes,
> Un enfant dans les fers. ... (I.2.251)

Pyrrhus also refers to the "murs fumants de Troie," echoing Virgil's "sol fumant." Andromaque's vision of Troy is both more personal and more tortured:

> *J'ai vu* mon père mort et nos murs embrasés;
> *Jai vu* trancher les jours de ma famille entière,
> Et mon époux sanglant traîné sur la poussière,
> Son fils seul avec moi, réservé pour les fers. (III.6.277)

This speech, like Pyrrhus', evokes the counterpoint of loss and salvage central to the play. Such references to Astyanax, sole remainder of Troy, punctuate the entire text.

> Astyanax, d'Hector jeune et malheureux fils;
> *Reste* de tant de rois sous Troie ensevelies. (I.1.247-48)
>
> Je passais jusqu'aux lieux où l'on garde mon fils ...
> Le seul bien qui me *reste* et d'Hector et de Troie. (I.4.254)
>
> Sauve tout ce qui *reste* et de Troie et d'Hector. (II.3.264)
>
> Mais il me *reste* un fils. (III.4.274)
>
> Il est du sang d'Hector, mais il en est le *reste*. (IV.1.284)

Andromaque evokes the image of the victors as well as that of the defeated: "Aux pieds des murs fumants de Troie / Les vainqueurs tout sanglants partageaient leur proie" (I.2.251). Obsessed by this great cataclysm, the characters entertain illusions of their role in it, as if they had a future as well as a past. In an impossible dream of return, Pyrrhus imagines Troy rising like a Phoenix from its ashes:

> Votre Ilion encor peut sortir de sa cendre;
> Je puis, en moins de temps que les Grecs ne l'ont pris,
> Dans ses murs relevés couronner votre fils. (I.4.256)
>
> On craint qu'avec Hector Troie un jour ne renaisse. (I.2.251)

But the fantasy of *Troie relevée* remains just that; its heritage will be retribution, not rebirth, salvage, not salvation. And all that can be salvaged is memory. The memory of Hector, which still strikes terror in the hearts of Greek wives and daughters:

> Ne vous souvient-il plus, seigneur, quel fut Hector?
> Nos peuples affaiblis s'en souviennent encor. (I.2.250)

And, of course, Andromaque's memory of Pyrrhus. While he undertakes to forget his past actions, she neither can nor will do so: "Dois-je les oublier, s'il ne s'en souvient plus?" In a central image of the play, she evokes her last changeless vision of Troy:

> Dois-je oublier mon père à mes pieds renversé,
> Ensanglantant l'autel qu'il tenait embrassé?
> Songe, songe, Céphise, à cette nuit cruelle
> Qui fut pour tout un peuple, une nuit éternelle;
> Figure-toi Pyrrhus, les yeux étincelants,
> Entrant à la lueur de nos palais brûlants,
> Et, de sang tout couvert, échauffant le carnage;
> Songe aux crise des vainqueurs, songe aux cris des mourants
> Dans la flamme étouffés, sous le fer expirants;
> Peins-toi dans ces horreurs, Andromaque éperdue. (III.8.280)

Andromaque's description, like Hermione's, is drawn from Book II of the *Aeneid*, in which Pyrrhus is condemned for his barbarism and sacrilege. In Robert Fitzgerald's translation, "Priam before the altars, with his blood drenching the fires that he himself had blessed" (50) clearly corresponds to Racine's "Ensanglantant l'autel qu'il tenait embrassé." But the differences are great. Aeneas' narration has all the impact of an eye-witness account: "I myself / *saw* Neoptolemus furious with blood / In the entrance way, and *saw* the two Atridae; / Hecuba I *saw*, and her hundred daughters." Andromaque was present as well at the massacre but her vision is a self-willed creation. It is an image, in the sense of Oreste's comments on the assassination of Pyrrhus:

> ... quoique mon courage
> Se fît de ce complot une funeste *image*
> J'ai couru vers le temple ... (V.3.296)

In *Britannicus*, Néron will use this same expression to refer to Junie: "Mais je m'en fais peut-être une trop belle image" (II.2). Andromaque's lines first contain the expression *songer*, which hovers between memory and imagination. But the verbs which appear later in the passage — *figure-toi*, and especially *peins-toi* — enter the domain of art, turning *souvenir* into *image*. In Racine, it is not the past itself which determines the future, but the picture the mind paints of it. And *An-*

dromaque literally paints herself into the center of a tableau of horrors. In the end, emptied of all emotion, she will become a figure of Memoria, a living monument to War;

> Andromaque au travers de mille cris de joie,
> Porte jusqu'aux autels le souvenir de Troie;
> Incapable toujours d'aimer et de haïr,
> Sans joie et sans murmure elle semble obéir. (V.2.294)

When memory is aesthetically immobilized — transformed into a tableau — all possibility of action is eliminated, leaving only reaction and retribution: playing back means paying back. As in the Greek tragedy, a kind of moral balance works through events of the utmost brutality. In this context Pyrrhus' famous line — "brûlé de plus de feux que je n'en allumai" — deserves more serious attention than it has received. Usually dismissed as a *précieux* wordplay, it shows syntactically the equilibrium of vengeance. Moreover, it is integrated into the central tragic imagery of fire and ashes. Like the references to Andromaque — "aux cendres d'un époux doit-elle enfin sa flamme" (129) — it reveals the connection of the characters to their past and to an implacable justice. Racine's version delineates the form of this justice more clearly than the Greek models. Euripides does talk of the old quarrels between the grandfathers of Hermione and Pyrrhus, Menelaus and Peleus, and suggests Oreste will be responsible for Pyrrhus' death; but Racine's *Andromaque* goes further. When Hermione paints a picture of Pyrrhus' guilt, she also suggests the future agents of its expiation: "De votre propre main Polyxène égorgée / Aux yeux de tous les Grecs *indignés contre vous*" (IV.4). In Virgil's account, there is no mention of any Greek indignation at Pyrrhus' actions, and, indeed, such a reaction appears implausible. But it allows Racine to foreshadow the wedding-turned-sacrifice at the altar, with Pyrrhus' former companions as sacrificers.

While the climax is foreshadowed to the audience, the participants remain ignorant of their roles, their fates and even the prefiguratory import of the words they speak. This paradox applies particularly to Oreste. From the outset, he explicitly brings the themes of destiny and divine vengeance to the fore:

> Oui, puisque je retrouve un ami si fidèle,
> Ma *fortune* va prendre une face nouvelle; ...
> Hélas! qui peut savoir le *destin* que m'amène?
> L'amour me fait ici chercher une inhumaine:

> Mais qui sait ce qu'il doit ordonner de mon *sort*,
> Et si je viens chercher ou la vie ou la mort? (I.1.247)

From beginning to end, Oreste conceives of his fate in terms of passion. He only sees, as some readers only see, the "love story": in Racine's wordplay, "Réunissons trois coeurs qui n'ont pu s'accorder." And it is in Oreste's final "mad" scene that his blindness to the moral dimension of his adventure is most apparent; a blindness exemplary of the entire dramatic world. The play reaches its climax with two speeches by Oreste, interrupted by Pylade's interjection, "Ah! seigneur!" (300-01). In his first speech, the dominant vocabulary of passion — *malheur, douleur, plaisir, misère, colère, content, joie, coeur* — seems out of keeping with the tragic events just narrated. The second speech does introduce those mythological instruments of vengeance, the Furies and the Harpies, but again, the context is romanticized — or at least eroticized. Pyrrhus is the romantic "rival," whom Hermione cruelly embraces before Oreste's eyes; and Oreste continues to offer her his heart — if only to be devoured. Until the end, Oreste persists in seeing himself as a hopeless victim of love, in no way responsible for his own fate.

> Oui, je te loue, ciel, de ta persévérance!
> Appliqué sans relâche au soin de me punir,
> Au comble des douleurs tu m'as fait parvenir.

Oreste's hallucinations are first heralded by a sudden attack of blindness: "Mais quelle épaisse nuit tout à coup m'environne?" This darkness gives way to a half-light, filled with nightmarish visions: "Grâce au ciel j'entrevoi ... / Dieux: quels ruisseaux de sang coulent autour de moi!" Finally, the obscurity is transformed into the infernal night of death: "Venez-vous m'enlever dans l'éternelle nuit?" This evocation recalls the last night of Troy, which, according to Andromaque, was also *une nuit éternelle*; but it also conveys Oreste's total ignorance of the moral order, of the great, fatal weights which balance and counterbalance all things. With the exception of Andromaque, who helps bring her own historical fate to fruition, this order is hidden from the characters. Ironically, despite the many hints given by Racine, it is often hidden from the audience as well, who persist in viewing Andromaque as Greek drama *habillé à la française*. Certainly Racine saw the need to "pretty up" his tragedy, to reduce its archetypal savagery, but the ferocity — and the fatality — are still there to be seen. Perhaps Racine's vision is not so far from Homer's invocation in the

Iliad; "sing, goddess, the anger of Pelius' son Achilles and its devastation" (I.1; trans. Lattimore 59). The destruction of Troy was the will of Zeus, enacted through human passion. This same instrumentality is represented in *Andromaque* through the words the characters say without full understanding, through the images they see without full sight.

In *Britannicus*, and in *Andromaque*, the image links fantasy to memory, duration to action. *Britannicus* is the story of Néron: a Néron who is not yet the criminal lunatic of historical tradition, but what Racine calls "un monstre naissant": a young man poised on the verge of his monstrous destiny. Néron did not inherit the throne legitimately, but was placed there by his wily mother Agrippine, who married the emperor Claudius in his old age and convinced him to disinherit his own son, Britannicus, before conveniently dying (probably poisoned by his wife). This whole seamy story is told in Tacitus' *Annals*, Racine's principal source. One could say that the play is created out of a tension between story and image; and in order to locate this tension, we must first examine the story — the plot — of *Britannicus*.

When *Britannicus* begins, Néron has governed Rome honorably for three years, under the watchful eye of his mother. But portents are not good. Agrippine fears her son is starting to resent her authority over his person and the state. To defend herself against this potential threat, Agrippine conspires to have Britannicus marry Junie, his childhood sweetheart and a relative of the imperial family. Néron interrupts the course of young love by having Junie abducted, which declenches the action of Racine's play. When the curtain rises, it is the middle of the night. Agrippine is lurking outside Néron's apartment, trying to get in to see him and find out the meaning of this abduction. At first, she interprets the act as a sign of her son's wickedness: "L'impatient Néron cesse de se contraindre; / Las de se faire aimer, il veut se faire craindre" (I.1.393). But his basic motive remains unclear to her: what does he want? Is he inspired by hate or love? Does he only seek the pleasure of hurting (*le plaisir de nuire*)? Or is he really trying to get at me, his mother, through them?

With her relentless questioning, Agrippine raises the basic dramatic issue of the play: what direction will Néron take? Will he continue in the path of virtue, or is the abduction of Junie a first step towards tyranny? This dramatic issue also implies an epistemological issue. From the beginning of the play, the characters (and, by extension, the audience) are looking for a truth, in this case a psychological truth.

All want to know what Néron is really like. Is he a weakling, a monster, or just misunderstood? Once this psychological diagnosis is made, his future acts can be deduced because, in this interpretive scheme, character causes action: we do what we do because of what we are. Conversely, action is a sign of character: to find out the truth about someone, we interpret the language of his acts. In the early scenes of *Britannicus*, Agrippine tries to "read" Néron in this way, looking through the abduction of Junie towards its underlying motives: "surprenons, s'il se peut, les secrets de son âme" (I.1.397). But Néron foils these attempts at "reading" by hiding the text: he remains secluded in his apartment throughout the first act.

At the beginning of act II, Néron emerges from hiding to give his own answer to these questions. Whatever his original reason for kidnapping Junie, after one look at her, "Néron est amoureux" (I.2.404). The emperor follows up this deliberately melodramatic statement by a description of Junie as she appeared to him that night, surrounded by her captors (see below, pp. 71-74). Néron wants Junie, but many obstacles stand in the way of his possessing her: Britannicus, Agrippine, his good repute among the people, and his wife Octavie. This last obstacle appears the least to Néron: he will simply divorce her. To get rid of Britannicus, Néron frames a more devious plan: he threatens to kill his rival if Junie does not discourage Britannicus' suit. In a refinement of sadism, Néron watches the conversation between the lovers from a hiding place. Junie knows he is watching, and although she loves Britannicus, she must pretend indifference to save his life. However, Néron's scheme is foiled when the lovers meet again in act III. The Emperor is not watching this time, and Junie can explain her previous coldness to Britannicus. This play of truth and falsehood reiterates an already familiar pattern. The false appearances created by Néron are dissipated to reveal an emotional truth: Junie's constant love for Britannicus.

When Néron finds the reconciled pair together, he is naturally furious. In a jealous rage, he has Britannicus arrested. At this point, the young man's fate appears sealed, but Néron still hesitates before the definitive act of murder. Finally, his evil advisor, Narcisse, convinces Néron that letting Britannicus live would be interpreted as a victory for Agrippine. Once again, an act constitutes a symbolic language which imposes its meaning on the actor as well as on his audience. In an attempt to free himself from symbols of his mother's influence, Néron orders the poisoning of Britannicus. But Junie escapes him and finds sanctuary with the vestal virgins. At the end of the play, a frustrated Néron foreshadows, by his furious looks, the criminal maniac he is now sure to become.

Summarized in this way, *Britannicus* reveals a variation on the classical concept of truth outlined above. That is, a basic reality (in this case, Néron's innate ferocity) lies hidden at the heart of the play, and expresses itself through words and deeds. Repressed by his early education and his mother's authority, Néron's ferocity lies dormant for a while. But eventually it must come out: lion cubs must grow into lions. The catalyst that releases Néron's pent-up criminality is his passion for Junie. Once this breach in the emotional dike has been made, Néron's hostility towards his half-brother and his mother are also released (she predicts her own death at the end of the play). Moreover, even when Néron's ferocity is disguised, it is already perceptible: for the observant, "certain signs" point to the face behind the mask.

This interpretation of *Britannicus* is satisfying — up to a point. But in order to arrive at it, I have smoothed over certain irregularities in the Racinian landscape. I now propose to examine one of these irregularities: a scene that is not there (or is no longer there). I am referring to V.6 in the first version of the play. In this scene, Junie originally came on stage after Britannicus' death, and Néron tried to console her: "Belle Junie, allez; moi-même je vous suis. / Je vais, par tous les soins que la tendresse inspire, / Vous ..." (1105 n.1). Néron's speech is interrupted by the arrival of his mother, who literally steps between her son and Junie, frustrating his desires for the last time.

Racine reports in his preface to *Britannicus* that spectators found this short scene very odd (*étrange* [386]). Why should Junie reappear after her lover has been murdered, much less speak to his murderer? And besides, the action is practically completed after Britannicus' death; why does Racine drag it on so long? As a result of these objections, V.6 was cut from later performances. But the question remains why Racine wrote it in the first place. The justification he gives in his preface is not very convincing: in ancient Greek drama, actors often came on stage just to say they were going from one place to another. In looking for a better explanation, I was drawn back towards the narration of Néron's first sight of Junie in II.2. This scene, which contains the most powerful poetry in the play, has been examined many times by critics.[3]

[3] For example, Serge Doubrovsky, "L'Arrivée de Junie dans *Britannicus*: la tragédie d'un scène à l'autre," *Littérature* 32 (1977) 27-54; Jules Brody, "Les Yeux de César,"

1 Excité d'un désir curieux,
Cette nuit je l'ai vue arriver en ces lieux,
Triste, levant au ciel ses yeux mouillés de larmes,
Qui brillaient au travers des flambeaux et des armes,
5 Belle, sans ornement, dans le simple appareil
D'une beauté qu'on vient d'arracher au sommeil.
Que veux-tu? je ne sais si cette négligence,
Les ombres, les flambeaux, les cris et le silence,
Et le farouche aspect de ses fiers ravisseurs,
10 Relevaient de ses yeux les timides douceurs.
Quoi qu'il en soit, ravi d'une si belle vue,
J'ai voulu lui parler, et ma voix s'est perdue:
Immobile, saisi d'un long étonnement,
Je l'ai laissé passer dans son appartement.
15 J'ai passé dans le mien. C'est là que, solitaire,
De son image en vain j'ai voulu me distraire:
Trop présente à mes yeux je croyais lui parler;
J'aimais jusqu'à ses pleurs que je faisais couler.
Quelquefois, mais trop tard, je lui demandais grâce:
20 J'employais les soupirs, et même la menace.
Voila comme, occupé de mon nouvel amour,
Mes yeux, sans se fermer, ont attendu le jour.
Mais je m'en fais peut-être une trop belle image;
Elle m'est apparue avec trop d'avantage:
Narcisse, qu'en dis-tu? (II.2.405)

This monologue encompasses the recital of two visions: the initial depiction of the "real" Junie, as she appeared to Néron the night before, later gives way to Néron's compelling visual fantasy of her. However, a simple distinction between fantasy and reality does not adequately describe the passage. The woman, Junie, never exists independently; both visions are "fictions" created in Néron's mind and evoked through words. Junie's fictional status is clear in the syntax of the passage. Only once, at the end of the text, is she allowed to become a grammatical subject (*Elle* [24]). Everywhere else, she is the direct object, the *l'*, the silent *e* of Néron's gaze (2). Similarly, two lines begin with "disembodied adjectives" (*Triste* [3]; and *Belle* [5]) which have no substantive referent in the passage. Lines 3 and 5 also reinforce another aspect of the text: its static, tableau-like quality. The

Studies in Seventeenth-Century French Literature, ed. J.-J. Demorest (Garden City: Anchor, 1966) 185-200; Jean Starobinski, "Racine et la poétique du regard," *L'Oeil vivant* (Paris: Gallimard, 1961) 69-90.

capture scene, occupying the first half (up to line 15), is structured on a series of oppositions which cancel one another out to produce an effect of stillness. For example, the perfectly balanced line 8, "Les ombres, les flambeaux, les cris et le silence," creates an effect reminiscent of classical painting — a Poussin "Rape of the Sabine Women." On a psychological level, this painterly representation reflects the essential coldness of Néron's erotic response: like Soames Forsythe in *A Man of Property*, Néron has the collector's eye.

Yet there is a more than esthetic distance separating beholder from beheld. While in her presence, Néron could not bring himself to speak to Junie (12). He lets the "real" woman disappear in order to transform her, in the second moment of his vision, from sight into image (*vue* [11]; *image* [16]) — an image which takes on a near-hallucinatory power. Alone in his room, Néron carries on whole conversations (or rather monologues) with the image he has created: "trop présente à mes yeux je croyais lui parler; / J'aimais jusqu'à ses pleurs que je faisais couler. / Quelquefois, mais trop tard, je lui demandais grâce: / J'employais les soupirs, et même la menace" (16-20). These lines contain the imperfect, a tense denoting repeated, continued and, in this case, obsessive activity. But their temporal referent is ambiguous: is Néron recalling or imagining? are the tears he caused to flow Junie's real tears, her imagined tears, or even, perhaps, the tears she will shed later on? All these allusions are present, in an abolition of time. For, as I will show, Néron's monologue contains not only a recollection of the past, but a preview of coming events. For example, in the very next scene, Néron uses both *soupirs* and *menaces* in an effort to win Junie. He sighs at her feet (*respirer à vos pieds*) but also warns her that if she turns him down she will regret it. Racine's language is naturally more elegant: "Et ne préférez point à la solide gloire / Des honneurs dont Cesar prétend vous revêtir, / La gloire d'un refus sujet au repentir" (II.3.412). When Britannicus appears in act III, Néro's threats become more open: "Si vous n'avez appris à vous laisser conduire, / Vous êtes jeune encore, et l'on peut vous instruire" (III.8.428).

As all these examples indicate, Néron's monologue performs a function of "poetic pre-enactment": it serves as a blueprint for future dramatic action. This notion helps solve the puzzle of the suppressed scene V.6. Junie must come back in that scene to fulfill the poetic prophecy contained in line 19 of the monologue from II.2. ("Quelquefois, mais trop tard, je lui demandais grâce.") When Néron asks Junie's forgiveness, it is certainly too late — Britannicus has been murdered at Néron's orders — but he must ask in order to show it is too late, and thereby close the fatal poetic circle opened in act II. In II.3, Néron almost parodies to Junie the words Narcisse had spoken to him just moments before: Narcisse's "Que présage à mes yeux cette tristesse obscure" (I.2.204) becomes Néron's "Lisez-vous dans mes yeux quelque triste présage?" (II.3.409). In fact, everyone's future is mirrored in Néron's eyes. This mirroring effect is reinforced by the borrowing of lines from Néron's monologue. Néron says of Britannicus, "Je me fais de sa peine une image charmante" (II.8.417), a clear echo of his reference to Junie, "Je m'en fais peut-être une trop belle image" (II.2.23, my line numbering). Junie also echoes Néron's lines without having heard them, saying to Britannicus: "Votre image sans cesse est présente à mon âme" (III.7.425). Compare Néron: "De son image en vain j'ai voulu me distraire. / Trop présente à mes yeux je croyais lui parler" (II.2.16-17). Agrippine's speeches also contain variations on Néron's monologue. For example, "J'essaierai tour à tour la force et la douceur" (423) paraphrases his "j'employais les soupirs et même la menace." As Racine remarked in the Seconde Préface to *Britannicus*: "Voici celle de mes tragédies que je puis dire que j'ai le plus travaillée" (389). Indeed, it is difficult to see these echoes and repetitions as other than deliberate; they point to Néron's monologue as a poetic center from which everything else in the play emanates.

To return, in conclusion, to our original question — whether the philosophers seek the same truth as the poets — the answer, for *Britannicus*, is yes and no. On the one hand, our analysis of the play's structure reveals little of the analytical-referential model of classical discourse. In the classical, Cartesian model, one arrives at knowledge through deduction — etymologically, the leading-out of concepts into a rational sequential order. In *Britannicus*, deduction is replaced by intuition — etymologically, seeing-in. In a moment of illumination, Néron, like the divinely crazed seer of Greek tragedy, both perceives the future and reveals it in his gaze. But this latter notion of truth is, by necessity, nondramatic; discourse reveals truth, but cannot produce it. To make *Britannicus* a drama, Racine must create the impression of plot development, of freedom, of unfolding time — all of which he does, on the whole, quite competently. Nevertheless, as Racine's audience correctly sensed, the play is "out of line" with the orderly unrolling of a dramatic plot. According to M. J. Muratore, "Racine's is essentially a theater of non-evolution; the characters travel over and over the same ground, ending precisely where they begin" ("Racinian Stasis" 114). From act II on, time in *Britannicus* resembles what Timothy Reiss calls, in his study of *Phèdre*, the "fabulous no-time" of myth and fable (*Truth and Tragedy* 277). In *Unspeakable Sentences*, Ann Banfield formulates a distinction between narration and representation which may be useful here. Narration, "telling" in the literal sense, is linear, numerical: "A telling, a counting, is a setting down in a linear order of discrete limits which need have no other relation to one another except that of a strict ordering" (264-65). Representation, on the other hand, "is first of all a picture, whether actual or mental. As such it is atemporal — the picture is always now" (268). Events and consciousness thus represent two kinds of knowledge, the models for both of which originated in the seventeenth century. Banfield's thesis complements Michael Black's assertion that poetic language bypasses some of the processes of conceptualization in order to "put us in contact, as direct as can be, with the movement of other minds" (Black 16). In this sense, *Britannicus* does fulfill the classical imperative to express thought: it does represent a poet's mind at work. But this mental process takes a very different form from Hobbes' train of thought, rolling down its narrow gauge track. Perhaps a more apt metaphor for Racine's achievement is suggested by the mathematical mystic Pascal, who defined eloquence as "un portrait de la pensée."

Poetic language, according to Leo Spitzer, produces "adumbrations of a metaphysical world" beyond everyday experience (*Language* 87). More than any other French classical playwright, Racine provides a testing ground for Spitzer's assertion. In Racine's secular plays, written during the first part of his career, the shadows cast by the metaphysical are dark indeed; the characters are trapped within physical and temporal bounds from which they cannot escape. This entrapment is metaphorically represented in some of the plays we have already examined. Thus, in *Britannicus*, the young hero is caught within the morbid gaze of the Emperor Néron which will ultimately provoke his destruction. In *Andromaque*, it is the chains of passion which entangle the characters and lead to their predetermined fate. Similar images of entrapment are present in other plays. In *Bajazet*, there are the tortuous corridors of the Turkish harem; in *Phèdre*, the windings of the Cretan labyrinth which enclosed Theseus, and the horses' reins that will fatally entangle his son. In the late biblical dramas *Esther* and *Athalie*, these bonds are finally dissolved as divine truth descends on Earth to rescue the characters from crime and error. *Iphigénie* represents a midpoint between these two visions. A love story in the *galant* seventeenth-century manner, it is also a play in which the supernatural assumes a predominant role. In the end, actors and audience alike become witnesses to a ceremony planned by the gods.

Racine accomplishes this sacralization by a return to the Greek inspiration of his earlier works. *Iphigénie*, like Euripides' *Iphigenia in Aulis*, begins in the dark. But while the Euripidean night, broken only by the guard's lantern, is complete and secretive, Racine's is a semi-obscurity, a darkness before the dawn. "A peine un faible jour vous éclaire et me guide," says Arcas at the beginning of I.1, and Agamemnon closes the scene with "Déjà le jour plus grand nous frappe et nous éclaire" (679). The repetition of the verb *éclairer*, in conjunction with *faible* and *guide*, sets the metaphysical boundaries of the play: the characters have just enough light to see that they cannot see.

Throughout *Iphigénie*, Racine continues to play on this paradoxical relation between ignorance and truth, causing Agamemnon to say to Iphigénie in IV.3, "Ma fille, il est trop vrai: j'ignore pour quel crime / La colère des dieux demande une victime:" (716). Agamemnon's avowal of ignorance forms a sinister pendant to that of Eriphile, Achille's enigmatic captive:

> J'ignore qui je suis; et, pour comble d'horreur,
> Un oracle effrayant m'attache à mon erreur,
> Et, quand je veux chercher le sang qui m'a fait naître,
> Me dit que sans périr je ne me puis connaître. (II.1.688)

Horreur/erreur: the assonance tells us that if truth is perilous, ignorance is more so. Eriphile's very fantasies are potentially destructive: believing she is a Trojan, she rationalizes that by betraying Iphigénie to the priest Calchas she would be performing a patriotic act:

> Quelle joie!
> Que d'encens brûlerait dans les temples de Troie,
> Si, troublant tous les Grecs, et vengeant ma prison,
> Je pouvais contre Achille armer Agamemnon ...
> Et si de tout le camp mes avis dangereux
> Faisaient à ma patrie un sacrifice heureux! (IV.1.713)

Ironically, it is Eriphile, not Iphigénie, who will perform a filial sacrifice; her patriotic aims will be fulfilled by her own death, which will allow the Greeks to rescue her mother, Helen.

Misled themselves, the characters also mislead one another. And their machinations add to the complexity — one could almost say confusion — of the action. If, as Aristotle claims, "the soul of tragedy is the plot" (*Poetics* 13), then *Iphigénie* has almost too much soul. Rather than a simple, orderly action, the play nearly explodes with a Baroque proliferation of incident. But if we examine the plot structure closely we discover that, to paraphrase Malebranche, nothing happens until God makes it happen. In the Euripidean version of the legend, Agamemnon lures Iphigenia to Aulis on the pretext of a marriage to Achille, and then tries to ward off her coming with a second letter. In act II of Racine's play, which has been called *l'acte des malentendus*, he adds several complications of his own. In Agamemnon's second letter, Racine has the King hint that Achille no longer desires to marry Iphigénie because he has fallen in love with Eriphile. The letter is not delivered in time because Iphigénie and Clytemnestre go astray on arrival in Aulis: "Arcas s'est vu trompé par notre égarement." When the letter finally is received, Agamemnon's false accusation arouses Iphigénie's jealous suspicions:

> Cet amant, pour me voir brûlant d'impatience,
> Que les Grecs de ces bords ne pouvaient arracher,
> Qu'un père de si loin m'ordonne de chercher,
> S'empresse-t-il assez pour jouir d'une vue
> Qu'avec tant de transports je croyais attendue? (II.3.694)

Agamemnon's stratagem also provokes a spirited but mistaken rivalry scene between the two young women in II.4.

For his part, Achille knows nothing of the alleged wedding and does not even realize Iphigénie has landed in Aulis until he encounters her in scene 6:

> Il est donc vrai madame, et c'est vous que je vois!
> Je soupçonnais d'erreur tout le camp à la fois.
> Vous en Aulide! vous! Eh! qu'y venez-vous faire?
> D'où vient qu'Agamemnon m'assurait le contraire?

To this ingenuous questioning, Iphigénie sarcastically replies: "Seigneur, rassurez-vous: vos voeux seront contents / Iphigénie encore n'y sera pas longtemps" [exit] (600). In this scene, Achille's ignorance creates a quasi-comic effect; great hero he may be, great practical psychologist he is not.

As the play progresses and the characters' ignorance persists, their actions take on a heightened air of gratuity. If act II is the act of misunderstandings, and act III of misrevelations, act IV might be called the act of red herrings. In IV.6, the audience's attention is diverted from Iphigénie's sacrifice to a power struggle between Agamemnon and Achille. The King had nearly decided to save Iphigénie; but offended by Achille's threats, he appears to reverse himself:

> Ma gloire intéressée emporte la balance.
> Achille menaçant détermine mon coeur;
> Ma pitié semblerait un effet de ma peur.
> Holà! gardes, à moi! (722)

But the threat raised by these lines never materializes; Agamemnon immediately changes his mind yet again and decides to save Iphigénie while separating her from Achille forever. This threatened rupture creates yet another *fausse piste*; when she hears of it, Iphigénie declares she would rather die. The ensuing scene with Achille recalls a *combat de gloire* between the same two characters in Rotrou's version of the play (III.333). It also calls up memories of Corneille's Chimène. But the surprise ending of Racine's *Iphigénie*, which Andrew Porter once called "Gilbertian," undercuts any potential for heroism. What could have been tragic is made comic — or, at most, tragicomic.

However, it is not necessary to anticipate Racine's *dénouement*; the gratuity of these scenes is conveyed through the language itself. For example, when Achille threatens to perform sacrilegious horrors at the altar, the very excess of his discourse renders it suspect. At the end of act III, Achille had stated: "Je perds trop de moments en des discours frivoles; / Il faut des actions, et non pas des paroles" (711). But like their paradigms in Cornelian drama, these lines only serve to remind us of the divorce between words and actions. This divorce is even more apparent in the images the characters create: each paints a different picture of Iphigénie's sacrifice, according to an intimate internal model. Thus, Achille's vision of blood-letting in III.6 betrays his own savage nature:

> C'est peu de vouloir, sous un couteau mortel,
> Me montrer votre coeur fumant sur un autel:
> D'un appareil d'hymen couvrant ce sacrifice,
> Il veut que ce soit moi qui vous mène au supplice,
> Que ma crédule main conduise le couteau,
> Qu'au lieu de votre époux je sois votre bourreau?
> Et quel était pour vous ce sanglant hyménée,
> Si je fusse arrivé plus tard d'une journée? (708)

In V.2, Achille's imaginings further evolve into an inverted fantasy of desecration which leaves the "real" sacrifice far behind:

Si de sang et de morts le ciel est affamé,
Jamais de plus de sang ses autels n'ont fumé.
A mon aveugle amour tout sera légitime:
Le prêtre deviendra la première victime;
Le bûcher, par mes mains détruit et renversé,
Dans le sang des bourreaux nagera dispersé;
Et si, dans les horreurs de ce désordre extrême,
Votre père frappé tombe et périt lui-même,
Alors, de vos respects voyant les tristes fruits,
Reconnaissez les coups que vous aurez conduits.
IPHIGÉNIE: Ah! seigneur! Ah! cruel! (728)

Leaving aside the "psychological" implications of Achille's speech, I wish to emphasize the sense of reality the passage manages to convey without really departing from the contingent. When Achille says, using the *passé composé*, "Jamais de plus de sang ses autels *n'ont* fumé," it is as though the violence has already taken place... but it has not.

Achille is not the only bloodthirsty character in the cast. As Gérard Defaux has shown, Iphigénie herself, in an exaltation of martyrdom, sees her own blood fertilizing the field of conquest of the Greeks:

Ce champ si glorieux ou vous aspirez tous,
Si mon sang ne l'arrose, est stérile pour vous....
Déjà Priam pâlit! Déjà Troie en alarmes
Redoute mon bûcher, et frémit de vos larmes.
Allez; et, dans ces murs vides de citoyens,
Faites pleurer ma mort aux veuves des Troyens.
(V.2.727; see also IV.3)

But it is Clytemnestre who demonstrates to the greatest degree what Malebranche calls "la communication contagieuse des imaginations fortes." In a famous speech in IV.4, Clytemnestre transforms her daughter's sacrifice into a symbolic rape:

Un prêtre, environné d'une foule cruelle,
Portera sur ma fille une main criminelle,
Déchirera son sein, et d'un oeil curieux,
Dans son coeur palpitant consultera les dieux!
Et moi, qui l'amenai triomphante, adorée,
Je m'en retournerai seule et désésperée!
Je verrai les chemins encor tout parfumés
Des fleurs dont sous ses pas on les avait semés! (718)

The trampled blossoms, like an image in an old silent film, reinforce the theme of "deflowering," while the reiteration of the first person singular (*et moi* ... *je* ... *je* ...) serves to remind us that this is not a description but an imaginative creation. The point about Racine's imagined *récits* is that, despite their evocatory power, none of them is ever enacted. By simple Aristotelian criteria, they are doubly removed from any mimetic function. Not only is the action they allude to — Iphigénie's sacrifice — never performed, but even this putative action serves only as a point of departure for the characters' own mental constructions. Further, the imagined *récits* are non-Aristotelian from a structural viewpoint because they have little or no effect upon the play's outcome. A comparison should make this point clearer. As we have seen, *Britannicus* also contains an imagined *récit*: Nero's famous narration of his first sight of Junie. But in Nero's case the *récit* has a direct relation to the action: the image of Junie, and the troubled feelings it evokes, cause the Emperor to encompass the destruction of the other characters and ultimately his own. In *Iphigénie*, by contrast, the causal connection between thought and event is severed. While the imagined *récits* constitute the dramatic soul of the play, they supply little motive power. In *Iphigénie*, it is as though the characters talk, and the audience listens, while all wait for the gods to act.

Conscious of their own ignorance and confusion, the characters attempt to *sortir d'erreur* by interrogating the gods. Thus, Eriphile, "de son destin, qu'elle ne connaît pas, / Vient, dit-elle, en Aulide interroger Calchas" (I.4.684). The principal means of interrogation is sacrificial augury, which is often referred to in a clandestine manner, as though it were in itself a guilty act: as Agamemnon says, "Je fis sur ses autels un secret sacrifice" (676). Interestingly, the sacrifice of Iphigénie, which in itself has no "informational" purpose, is also assimilated to a ritual of augury. Achille uses the expression: "me montrer votre coeur fumant sur un autel" (708), and Clytemnestre, in the speech quoted above, carries this image much further:

> Un prêtre, environné d'une foule cruelle,
> Portera sur ma fille une main criminelle,
> Déchirera son sein, et, d'un oeil curieux,
> Dans son coeur palpitant consultera les dieux!
> (IV.4.718)

These lines refer to a standard practice of animal sacrifice described by Homer and other ancient authors, and summarized by Walter Burkert in *Homo necans*: "The heart, sometimes still beating, is put on the altar. A seer is present to interpret the lobes of the liver" (6).

Neither Aeschylus nor Euripides refers to Iphigenia's sacrifice in this way. It is a "straight" human sacrifice, if one may use this expression, with no augury involved. Euripides' *Electra*, however, which Racine had reread and annotated prior to composing *Iphigénie*, does contain a graphic description of sacrificial augury. Orestes has returned to Argos in the guise of a stranger, to avenge his father's death. Aegisthus, not recognizing Agamemnon's son, asks him to participate in the sacrifice of a calf. After Aegisthus has slit the animal's throat, Orestes disembowels it: "Holding the beast by its foot, he laid the white flesh bare with one pass of the hand... and loosened the soft belly. Aegisthus scooped the prophetic viscera up in his hands. The liver lobe was not there. Unhidden, the portal-vein and gall-sac showed disaster coming at him even as he peered" (221.822-29). The imminent disaster, of course, is Aegisthus' own murder at Orestes' hands during the very sacrifice. Limited by classical notions of decorum, Racine cannot talk of portal-veins and gall-sacs; but in both plays exposure — the brutal unveiling of tender flesh — is related to *dis*closure. Racine's cruel insight reveals a link between sacrifice and torture. Both are violent forms of the search for knowledge — attempts to wrest the truth from its unwilling host.

But in *Iphigénie* the characters are enlightened only at the moment, and in the manner, of the gods' and the playwright's choosing. It is not until the play is nearly over that the characters are allowed to feel and recognize the cosmic forces ranged against them. When Clytemnestre and Iphigénie try to flee, they are turned back by the soldiers, like sacrificial animals trying to escape the pyre. Clytemnestre laments, "Hélas! je me consume en impuissants efforts, / Et rentre au trouble affreux dont à peine je sors. / Mourrai-je tant de fois sans sortir de la vie!" (731). To the elemental force of destiny, the Greek soldiers come to form a human adjunct. In V.2, they are themselves compared to the ocean waves which keep the army prisoner in Aulis, as though both are now ranged on the same side. Achille optimistically declares to Iphigénie, "Paraissez, et bientôt, sans attendre mes coups, / Ces *flots* tumulteux s'ouvriront devant vous" (726). But in the next scene, Eurybate asks anxiously:

> Achille, à qui tout cède, Achille à cet *orage*
> Voudrait lui-même en vain opposer son courage:
> Que fera-t-il, madame? et qui peut dissiper
> Tous les *flots* d'ennemis prêts à l'envelopper? (V.3.729)

Finally, in a moment of visionary exaltation in V.4, Clytemnestre reveals who is really responsible: "C'est le pur sang du dieu qui lance le tonnerre ... / J'entends gronder la foudre, et sens trembler la terre: / Un dieu vengeur, un dieu fait retentir ces coups" (731).[4] This vision will be confirmed by Ulysse in his final *récit*, in almost the same words: "Les dieux font sur l'autel entendre le tonnerre ..." (734). It is true that Arcas' speech appears to transfer this divine aura to Achille: "N'en doutez point, madame, un dieu combast pour vous. / Achille, en ce moment, exauce vos prières." But this hyperbole, designed to make aristocratic hearts beat faster, fails to chime with other reports. In V.5 we learn that Achille's attack has a delaying effect at best: "Achille est à l'autel. Calchas est éperdu. / Le fatal sacrifice est encore suspendu" (732). And in the final analysis, Achille's intervention is as destructive as it is constructive, because it creates a dangerous division in the army: "Déjà sur tout le camp la discorde maîtresse / Avait sur tous les yeux mis son bandeau fatal, / Et donné du combat le funeste signal ... Déjà coulait le sang, prémices du carnage" (733). It is not Achille, but the seer Calchas, who prevents the slaughter, at a moment carefully chosen by the god (and Racine): "Le dieu qui *maintenant* vous parle par ma voix, / M'explique son oracle, et m'instruit de son choix." Thus, despite Racine's efforts to raise him rhetorically to a superhuman level, Achille plays only a secondary role in the *dénouement*. It is Calchas who orders the sacrifice, and Eriphile who performs it.

"L'heureux personnage d'Eriphile," as Racine called her, is "heureux" (fortunate) for the playwright because she allows him, for once, to reconcile humanity with the gods. By a sort of dramatic Manichaeism, Racine concentrates all the evil in the play within one infernal character: "O monstre, que Mégère en ses flancs a porté! / Monstre que dans nos bras les enfers ont jeté!" (V.4.731). Once the source of evil is removed, the universe will be purified.[5] Eriphile further exonerates the gods by taking her own life. She self-destructs by the force of her own fatality: "Sous un nom emprunté sa noire *destinée* et *ses propres fureurs* ici l'ont amenée" (733). Eriphile's *fureurs*, like Hermione's and Phèdre's, arise from frustrated passion, and all these plays recall the account of Dido's madness and self-immolation in Book IV

[4] In Rotrou's *Iphigénie*, where Racine found this epithet, the god referred to is Zeus. Iphigénie, through her father, is descended from the gods: "du sang de Jupiter issu de tous côtés." By implication, Jupiter, reluctant to sacrifice his own blood, lights instead upon the expendable Eriphile. But while this supposition appears plausible, it is never explicitly confirmed in Racine's text.

[5] Cf. Gérard Defaux, "Violence et passion dans l'*Iphigénie* de Racine," *PFSCL* 11.21 (1984) 685-715, and René Girard, *La Violence et le sacré* (Paris: Grasset, 1972).

of the *Aeneid*. After Aeneas had abandoned her, Dido had a pyre built, ostensibly to burn the things her lover had left behind. Then she "ran to the innermost court of the palace, climbed the lofty pyre, frantic at heart, and drew Aeneas' sword" (100). If we compare this passage to Racine's description of Eriphile's suicide: "Furieuse, elle vole, et sur l'autel prochain, / Prend le sacré couteau, le plonge dans son sein" (734), many parallels appear: ran/*vole*, frantic at heart/*Furieuse*, sword/*couteau*. Racine retains both Virgil's eroticism and his moral, which could apply to all four unhappy heroines (Dido/Hermione/Eriphile/Phèdre): "Excess of love, to what lengths you drive our human hearts!" (93).

Through Eriphile's intervention, the question posed by Clytemnestre in IV.4 — "Le ciel, le juste ciel, par le meurtre ignoré, / Du sang de l'innocence est-il donc altéré?" — is shown to be rhetorical: the gods' justice was never seriously at issue. Ironically, the very belief in the gods' iniquity becomes a sign of human ignorance and frailty. For it is the weak characters who try to evade responsibility by blaming heaven. Stylistically, Racine communicates this form of bad faith through dependent clauses "laid upon" the characters. Thus, Agamemnon says to his daughter: "Faites rougir ces dieux qui vous ont condamnée" (716), and to Achille, in almost the same formula, "Plaignez-vous donc aux dieux qui me l'ont demandée" (720). Similarly, Eriphile declares in self-justification, "Consultons des fureurs qu'autorisent les dieux" (713). Each character projects on the supernatural the image of his or her needs and weaknesses. As Clytemnestre says to her husband, Agamemnon worships his own gods (IV.4.717).

By ascribing the guilt in the play to human weakness rather than divine will, Racine makes the gods appear perhaps more virtuous than before, but no more comprehensible. Calchas' justification for the sacrifice of the second Iphigénie is hardly any clearer than for the first. He simply states: "Elle me voit, m'entend, elle est devant vos yeux; / Et c'est elle, en un mot, que demandent les dieux." And the psychological element Racine introduces does not supply a complete explanation: we may know on a human level why Eriphile chooses to kill herself, but not why the gods willed her to die. In contrast, earlier authors tried harder to make the gods' ways intelligible to man. In Ovid's *Metamorphoses*, for example, we are told that a cloud was cast over the scene and a stag substituted for Iphigenia: "Thus when Diana was appeased by this more fitting victim, the wrath of the sea subsided along with that of the goddess..." (292). In Racine's version,

Ovid's goddess-in-the-cloud is downgraded to a hearsay report from a common soldier: "Le soldat étonné dit que dans une nue / Jusque sur le bûcher Diane est descendue" (734). We are told that the supernatural forces have been satisfied — *les dieux sont contents*, *le ciel est apaisé* — but not which ones or why.

Perhaps a more literal mythological presence might have offended the classical sense of *vraisemblance*; but in *Phèdre* Racine does not hesitate to have the gods play a direct role. More profoundly, Racine's restriction of the supernatural to its perceptible effects — the wind blowing, the sea moving, the pyre lighting of its own accord — conserves the mystery of the divine. Even the final epiphany remains external and partial: "Le ciel brille d'éclairs, s'entre'ouvre, et parmi nous / Jette une sainte horreur qui nous rassure tous" (734). The power and mysteriousness of the gods create an irreducible tension, conveyed through paradox and oxymoron (*sainte horreur qui rassure*). What results is a cosmic vision in which the gods appear awesome and powerful, humans weak and confused. For Racine, unlike Sophocles, the hero's blindness abnegates his moral responsibility; but it also reduces his heroic stature. Thus, Agamemnon, vacillating until the end, abdicates any control over events: "Le triste Agamemnon, / qui n'ose l'avouer, / Pour détourner ses yeux des meurtres qu'il présage, / Ou pour cacher ses pleurs, s'est voilé le visage" (732). *Triste*, as an epithet for the warrior Agamemnon, is both shocking and pathetic. Unlike the self-blinding of Oedipus, which is a sign of clairvoyance and moral courage, Agamemnon's *voile* is an insignium of defeat, a passive counterpart of the *bandeau de la discorde* which descends on the eyes of the combattants in V.2.

It is the impression of human blindness, rather than any explicit doctrinal content, which tempts critics to keep applying the label "Jansenist" to Racine.[6] Most of his characters are not fallen spiritually in an Augustinian sense; indeed, Achille and Iphigénie are almost sterling examples of virtue. But they cannot save themselves through their own efforts; above all, they cannot know anything unless the gods choose to enlighten them. It is the intellectual insufficiency of Racine's characters, rather than any moral weakness, which links his vision to Pascal's: "L'homme n'est qu'un sujet plein d'erreur naturelle, et ineffaçable sans la grâce. Rien ne lui montre la vérité. Tout l'abuse" (*Pensées* 45). Like the watchman at the beginning of Aeschylus'

[6] Cf. Philippe Sellier, "Le Jansénisme des tragédies de Racine: reálité ou illusion?" *CAIEF* 31 (1979) 135-48.

Agamemnon, the Racinian hero is waiting for "some godsend burning through the dark" (106.22-23). And yet the difference is great. In Aeschylus there remains a sense that despite the present darkness, enlightenment will be achieved by inner growth: "Zeus has led us on to know, / the Helmsman lays it down as law / that we must suffer, suffer into truth" (177-79). In Racine, truth, at best, is an enigmatic glimmer from above.

In *Iphigénie*, this religious vision determines its own dramatic form. As in Genet's *Les Nègres* or Beckett's *En attendant Godot*, one has the impression that action on stage mainly serves to divert attention from the more significant events taking place elsewhere. Racine's gods, like Godot, live in parts unknown. Moreover, the miraculous off-stage *dénouement* of *Iphigénie* prefigures in unredeemed, pagan form, the climactic chorus of *Esther*: "Dieu descend et revient habiter parmi nous: Cieux, abaissez-vous!" (III.9.861). When that descent occurs, the human drama as we know it will end, and Racine's characters, in a sense, are awaiting that end. Thus, while agreeing with Eléonore Zimmermann that *Iphigénie* has much in common with a Baroque tragicomedy, I interpret this commonality somewhat differently (Zimmermann 80). Rather than saying that *Iphigénie*, as a tragicomedy, has no metaphysics, or only plays with metaphysics, I would argue it teaches us something about the metaphysics of tragicomedy. A tragicomedy is not, as the common definition has it, "a tragedy with a happy ending"; in fact, it is not a tragedy at all. In a play where resolution is imposed from above, where little or no autonomy is granted to the characters, tragedy cannot occur. *Iphigénie* transcendent? perhaps; but her transcendence takes place on a Baroque stage, where a weak and misguided humanity wanders beneath an awesome and mysterious heaven.

"When first I knew you, you raised me up, so that I might see that there was something to see, but I was not yet able to see it. You beat back my feeble sight, sending down your beams most strongly upon me... I found myself to be far from you in a region of unlikeness." This passage from Book Seven of Augustine's *Confessions* (VII.x) evokes in spatial terms an experience of metaphysical displacement. After a brief glimpse of ultimate being, Augustine is thrown back into the ordinary physical world, which he now perceives as a place of exile, a *regio dissimilitudinis* where nothing resembles God. In "Saint Augustine's Region of Unlikeness: The Crossing of Exile and Language," Margaret Ferguson takes Augustine's "metaphysical exile" as the exemplary condition of all writing. Exile is "a central figure in the text's meditation on its own mode" (842) because signs are always removed from the truth; they can never express an ultimate meaning but only represent it, metaphorically, in dissimilitude. The writer, moreover, like the Augustinian exile, knows his loss; he nostalgically longs for some prelapsarian oneness with the Word, gone from us our present fallen state.

As we have seen, this yearning for an elusive truth, briefly glimpsed only to be lost in the shadows, permeates Racinian drama. He shares Augustine's suspicion of the sign: a Platonic conviction that nothing can be discerned with certainty because language itself is saturated with error. This implicit skepticism is raised in *Phèdre* to a conscious level: the protagonists themselves experience a metaphysical discomfort, an uneasy feeling that they are not seeing what there is to see. Thus, Theseus, gazing at his son's countenance, muses: "Et ne devrait-on pas à des signes certains/ Reconnaître le coeur des perfides humains!" (IV.2.784). Ironically, the innocence he sees in Hippolytus' face *is* a *signe certain*; it is his own flawed perceptions which prevent him from recognizing the truth until it is too late.

When Racine returns to the stage ten years later with *Esther*, we appear to have entered a different world. "Dieu tient le coeur des rois entre ses mains puissantes; / Il fait que tout prospère aux âmes innocentes, / Tandis qu'en ses projets l'orgeuilleux est trompé" (*Esther* I.1.818). God, Esther firmly declares, is with His people; in the colloquial phrase, He is "there" for them as a protective and redeeming presence, to see that the righteous prosper and the wicked are punished. Above all, He will mediate his exiles' return to the promised land. Thus, *Esther*, often dismissed as a "pièce pour jeunes filles" or a preliminary exercise for *Athalie*,[7] represents Racine's utopic attempt to make God and truth manifest on stage.

[7] Deprecatory judgments on *Esther* are legion. To give a few modern examples, Albert Cook calls it "a children's play for adults" (*French Tragedy: The Power of Enactment* [Chicago: Swallow, 1981] 28). According to John Lapp, "*Esther* is a slight play, rather quickly passed over by most critics" (*Aspects of Racinian Tragedy* [Toronto: University of Toronto Press, 1955] 31). Claude Abraham's comments, while still reserved, are more positive: "*Esther* may be just a school girl's exercise, but it marks the transition to a totally different sphere of inspiration. When Racine saw the dramatic potential of that and incorporated it into the system that had allowed him to write *Phèdre*, he created *Athalie*, one of the great plays of all time" (*Jean Racine* [Boston: Twayne, 1977] 143).

At first glance, the story of Esther appears a most unlikely vehicle for this undertaking. Esther has always occupied a marginal place in Scripture. According to S. R. Driver, "the spirit of Esther is not that which prevails in the Old Testament" (480). Samuel Sandmel states more forthrightly: "It is a light book, a ribald and funny story featuring concubines and drunken parties — hardly topics which lend themselves to meditation" (497). Even in an expurgated version suitable for the young girls at St. Cyr, the Book of Esther remains intrinsically secular. Religious practice is barely mentioned, the name of God not even pronounced. Offended by these lacks, the early Greek translators went so far as to introduce into the text the prayers that Esther should properly have said.[8]

Racine, like the Greek interpolators, apparently felt the need to deepen the religious import of his source. He did so by drawing on a whole biblical substrate which is only tangentially related to the Book of Esther: the story of the Babylonian exile. As recounted in Kings 25 and 2 Chronicles 36, the Babylonians destroyed the temple and city of Jerusalem in 587-586 B.C.E. and carried the Judean King away in chains. The exiled Judeans retained their traditions and identity and continually longed to return to their homeland. They were allowed to do so approximately 75 years later, after the conquest of Babylonia by the Persians (cf. Isaiah 45). Unlike the story of Esther, which is basically an entertaining folktale, the Babylonian exile is an event of great significance for the development of Judaism and, by extension, of Christianity. "The character of the religion of Israel changed decisively during and because of the Babylonian exile... it underwent a transition from the Hebrew religion to its offspring Judaism" (Sandmel 125). Moreover, from Augustine to Dante, the theme of the Babylonian exile has been one of the wellsprings of reflection on spiritual alienation. Like the Prodigal Son in the Far Country and the Wandering Jew in the desert, the Babylonian exile is removed from his proper place, cut off from the light. The fall from grace is

[8] These are extra-biblical chapters to the Hebrew Bible. They were incorporated in Roman Catholic Bibles as Appendices or marked within the text. Protestant Bibles consider the additions to the book of *Esther* as apocrypha. See Sandmel 497 and the Introduction to *Esther*, tr. Carey A. Moore (Garden City: Doubleday, 1971), *The Anchor Bible* 7B xxxii-xxxiii. Racine no doubt also was familiar with the edition and commentaries of Le Maistre de Sacy, but Sacy's presentation of "types" or analogies between the Old Testament and the New is not the subject of the present essay, which explores a region outside scriptural criticism in the traditional sense.

also a fall into language: a long-standing interpretive tradition identifies Babylon with Babel, so that Dante, for example, refers to the river of Babylon of Psalm 137 as the "waters of confusion" (*flumina confusionis*). The one Word is replaced by the clamor of tongues. Racine, by grafting this powerful theme onto the Estherian base, fundamentally alters the focus of his play.

In the process, Racine takes certain liberties with biblical history. He states in the preface to *Esther* that the King Ahasuerus is Darius (522-486 B.C.), a "good" Persian who helped the Jews reconstruct the temple at Jerusalem. Modern scholarship has established that the King in *Esther* is not Darius but his son, Xerxes I (486-465 B.C.). In addition, the composition of Esther dates from a later period, long after the original exile and return. "The words, there is a certain people scattered abroad and dispersed among the people in all the provinces of our kingdom (3:8) show that the dispersion had already for long been an accomplished fact."[9] The political issue in *Esther* is no longer the return of the dispossessed exiles, but the security of an ethnic and religious minority living amid hostile neighbors. To some extent, Racine's anachronisms reflect the historical beliefs of his time; but when he has Esther call the young Israelites "compagnes autrefois de ma captivité" he is stretching the bounds of historicity, even for his own epoch. Another change he makes is more subtle: Racine's biblical allusions have the effect of assimilating Darius to his grandfather Cyrus, a much more important figure who played a central role in the Babylonian exile. According to Deutero-Isaiah, Cyrus was God's principal instrument in accomplishing the exiles' return and the rebuilding of the Temple: "I have raised him up for victory and all his ways will I make straight / He will rebuild My city and send away My people from exile" (Isaiah 45:13). Historically, Racine's Ahasuerus may be Darius, but poetically he is Cyrus. This telescoping of biblical history places the theme of exile at the center of the Esther story.

Thus, despite his prefatory declarations that the word of Scripture is sacrosanct,[10] Racine has operated a profound reordering of bibli-

[9] *Dictionary of the Bible*, ed. James Hastings (New York: Scribner's, 1963) 269. The entry also states, "the language of *Esther* points unmistakably to a late date," probably the first half of the second century B.C.E. Esther is the only text of which there were no fragments found among the Dead Sea Scrolls, also indicating a late date. See also *Esther*, *Anchor Bible* lvii-lx.

[10] "... il me sembla que, sans altérer aucune des circonstances tant soit peu considérables de l'Ecriture sainte, ce qui serait, à mon avis, une espèce de sacrilège,

cal themes. Racine's *Esther* emerges from a creative reading of the Bible, just as his *Iphigénie* arose from a reading of Virgil and Euripides. It is this "re-reading" of Scripture that leads Racine to transform a Persian *fait-divers* into a drama of cosmic reconciliation. But Racine's reconciliation goes further still. As an examination of the text will show, *Esther* allows Racine finally to reunite biblical inspiration with the Greek.

In the beginning of *Esther*, the world is dislocated – nothing remains in its proper place. Racine immediately creates this sense of dislocation by placing the action within the framework of the Babylonian exile. Esther requests the chorus in I.2: "Mes filles, chantez-nous quelqu'un de ces cantiques / Où vos voix si souvent se mêlant à mes pleurs / De la triste Sion célèbrent les malheurs" (820-21). This speech contains clear echoes of Psalm 137: "By the waters of Babylon, there we sat down and wept, when we remembered Zion. On the willows there we hung up our lyres. For there our captors required of us songs, and our tormentors, mirth, saying, *Sing us one of the songs of Zion*! How shall we sing the Lord's song in a foreign land?" (1-4).[11] The psalmist's query raises a double issue: not only is it painful to recall the homeland in exile, but it is difficult, perhaps impossible, to use sacred language outside the sacred territory. In *Esther*, as in the Psalm, Jerusalem is portrayed as the lost and sacred land. "O rives du Jourdain! ô champs aimés des cieux!" (821). The image *champs aimés des cieux*, daring by classical standards, syntactically conveys an edenic union of God and nature: sky touches earth in a closed, protective embrace. Furthermore, the land itself bears traces of divine visitation. "Sacrés monts, fertiles vallées, / Par cent miracles signalées!" In the pre-exilic Zion, the signs of God unlike the signs of man, are manifest.

This pre-exilic past is recalled within the present context of its antithesis, the destruction of Jerusalem: "Tu n'es plus que poussière, et de cette grandeur / Il ne nous reste plus que la triste memoire." To the human grief of the Psalmist, Racine adds in the next lines a more abstract and spiritual lostness, a Pascalian tonality of *grandeur* and *misère*: "Sion, jusques au ciel élevée autrefois, / Jusqu'aux enfers maintenant abaissée." In both *Esther* and the biblical texts, the specific anti-image to the pre-exilic, holy Jerusalem is the destruction of the Temple. Psalm 137:7 states dramatically, "Remember, O Lord, against

je pourrais remplir toute mon action avec les seules scènes que Dieu lui-même, pour ainsi dire, a préparées" (601).

[11] References to the Bible are drawn from the Revised Standard Version.

the Edomites the day of Jerusalem, how they said, 'Rase it, rase it! Down to its foundations!'" Racine, more elegiac in tone, evokes the present desolation with an image of almost archaeological sparseness: "Sion, repaire affreux de reptiles impurs, / Voit de son temple saint les pierres dispersées, / Et du Dieu d'Israël les fêtes sont cessées."

Euripedes' *Trojan Women*, in the French version, is also filled with evocations reaching back to Homer and forward to Racine. "Voici déserts les lieux sacrés. Les sanctuaires ruissellent de sang ... O temples des dieux, ô ville chérie livrés à la mort par la lance et la torche ... Balayée vers le ciel, la cendre s'élève en poussière et me cache la place où était mon palais" (764:1315-26). And in Poseidon's prologue dedicated to his lost city: "Ce n'est plus à présent qu'une ruine fumante." This last passage also recalls the lines from the *Aeneid* cited earlier: "... que tout ce qui avait été Troie bâtie par Neptune ne fut plus qu'un sol fumant, les signes que nous donnèrent les dieux nous poussèrent à chercher de lointains exils dans un monde désert (*diversa exilia et desertas quaerere terras auguriis agimur diriom*)" (III.1-6). Racine finds and recreates the same tonalities of destruction and exile he had already called forth in *Andromaque*; but here they will be transfigured by a biblical vision.

These images of physical desolation are poetically associated a few lines later with the human dispersal of the exiles. Esther and her companions, like the temple stones, are scattered: "Jeunes et tendres fleurs par le sort agitées, / Sous un ciel étranger comme moi transplantées" (819); "Du doux pays de nos aïeux serons-nous toujours exilées?" (821). Finally, echoing the Psalmist, Racine's exiles state their firm resolve never to forget: "Puissé-je demeurer sans voix, / Si dans mes chants ta douleur retracée / Jusqu'au dernier soupir n'occupe ma pensée!" ["Let my tongue cleave to the roof of my mouth, if I do not remember you, if I do not set Jerusalem above my highest joy!"] (Psalms 137:6). Thus, from the beginning, Racine establishes the distinctive spiritual duality of exile: presence in absence, recollection in dispersion.

Racine, like the Old Testament prophets, is less concerned with the historical fact of exile than its underlying religious significance. "Why is the land ruined so that no one passes through? And the Lord says: Because they have forsaken my law which I set before them, and have not obeyed my voice, or walked in accord with it..." (Jeremiah 9:12-14). The parallel is clear: if the exiles have been turned away from Jerusalem, it is because they themselves first turned away from

God. Specifically, they have slid back into polytheism, the adulterous worshipping of foreign gods. Racine puts forth this interpretation in Esther's prayer in I.4:

> Hélas! ce peuple ingrat a méprisé ta loi;
> La nation chérie a violé sa foi,
> Elle a répudié son époux et son père
> Pour rendre à d'autres dieux un honneur adultère;
> Maintenant elle sert sous un maître étranger. (824-25)[12]

While most of Esther's prayer is drawn from the Greek interpolations, the comparison of polytheism to adultery is common throughout the prophets. We read, for example, in Jeremiah: "And I thought you would call me, My Father, and would not turn from following me. Surely, as a faithless wife leaves her husband, so have you been faithless to me, O house of Israel, says the Lord" (3:19-20). Other passages are more explicit: "Because harlotry was so light to her, she polluted the land, committing adultery with every stone and tree" (3:9). Idolatry — the perverse worshipping of images carved from stone or wood — is an act of desecration which defiles the holy land and makes it into a desert — Racine's "repaire affreux de reptiles impurs."[13]

Thus, already within the original Hebraic vision, the exiles' punishment symbolically fits their crime. The physical displacement of the Judeans responds to their spiritual alienation: they must serve a foreign master because they have worshipped foreign gods (*dei alieni*, Racine would have read in the Vulgate). The playwright incorporates this concept into his own, somewhat different, symbolic structure. While the Old Testament emphasizes the human alienation of affection and trust implicit in the breaking of the Covenant, Racine's alienation is tantamount to a whole-scale intellectual and spiritual fall. He

[12] See *Daniel, Esther and Jeremiah: The Additions*, ed. Carey A. Moore (Garden City: Doubleday, 1977); *The Anchor Bible* 44.

[13] This imagery belongs to the general category Northrop Fry calls "demonic": "the world of the nightmare and the scapegoat, of bondage and pain and confusion... the world also of perverted or wasted work, ruins and catacombs..." (*Anatomy of Criticism* [Princeton: Princeton University Press, 1971] 147). Animals are "monsters or birds of prey... the vulture, the cold and earthbound serpent... the demonic society is represented by Egypt and Babylon..." (149).. The archetypal antithesis to the demonic is the apocalyptic: the City, the Temple, the tree of life. In *Esther*, Racine draws on both sets of images.

appears to accept Augustine's definition of evil as a metaphysical *détournement*: "And when I asked myself what wickedness was I saw that it was not a substance but a swerving of the will which turns towards lower things and away from you (*detortae in infima voluntatis perversitatem proicientis intima sua*)" (*Confessions*, Book Seven XVI.150). In *Esther*, exile, idolatry and adultery are symbolically linked because they all represent humanity's wandering from the truth.

This spiritual alienation finds its exemplar in Ahasuerus, the *maître étranger* who possesses power without vision. As a king, Ahasuerus shows nearly divine attributes:

> Sur ce trône sacré qu'environne la foudre,
> J'ai cru vous voir tout prêt à me réduire en poudre.
> Hélas! sans frissonner, quel coeur audacieux
> Soutiendrait les éclairs qui partaient de vos yeux.
> Ainsi du dieu vivant la colère étincelle ... (II.7.839)

But he mistakes physical for spiritual power, turning towards the wrong source of light: "O soleil! ô flambeau de lumière immortelle!" And as he fails to distinguish between real and false gods, he also fails to discern good from evil, truth from lies. His convictions about Haman are as strong and as erroneous as his religious beliefs: "Je sais combien est pur le zèle qui t'enflamme: / Le mensonge jamais n'entra dans tes discours, / Et mon intérêt seul est le but où tu cours" (II.5.836).

This radical blindness would appear to bode the worst. But in *Esther* — and this distinguishes it from Racine's "pagan" plays — blindness is not irreparable, nor error universal. Even in a foreign land, the chosen people maintains indirect contact with the truth. This divine wisdom *in absentia* is represented by Mordecai, Esther's uncle and guide: "*Absent, je le consulte* et ses réponses sages / Pour venir jusqu'à moi trouvent mille passages" (I.1.819). Their mysterious access to knowledge gives Esther and her people the legitimacy of a government in exile. But to protect their knowledge, they must hide it. In the Book of Esther, as in Racine's play, the Queen's ancestry is kept secret. She "had not showed her people nor her kindred" (Esther 2:10), "je vins, mais je cachai ma race et mon pays" (818). The reasons for this secrecy differ. In the Old Testament, it has the basically practical aim of protecting Esther and her people from persecution. Racine adds another level of meaning, merging the secret with the sacred: Esther becomes a figure of truth which must be hidden until the moment arrives for its unveiling. Ahasuerus himself presents Esther in this light when he asks her to hide in the council chamber: "Venez, derrière un voile écoutant leurs discours / De votre propre clarté me prêter le secours" (841). This image recalls the paradoxes of Augustinian epistemology: knowledge, when lodged with error, must cover itself to shine through.

This notion of truth in exile brings another spatial dimension into Racine's spiritual landscape. Between the sacred land and the region of confusion, he inserts the halfway house of sanctuary. In his preface, Racine himself presents the story of Esther as a symbol for truth-in-the-world. When the authorities at St. Cyr asked him to write a play, "Je leur proposai le sujet d'Esther, qui les frappa d'abord, cette histoire leur paraissant pleine de grandes leçons d'amour de Dieu, et *de détachement du monde au milieu du monde même*" (812, my italics). Esther herself was raised in retreat: "On m'élévait alors, solitaire et cachée" (I.1.818). At the Persian court, she sets about establishing for her people a special space, a kind of sacred island in profane territory. In I.2, this sanctuary-like space is created on stage by the young girls themselves who gradually form a charmed circle around Esther. The stage directions are explicit:

> UNE DES ISRAÉLITES *chante derrière le théâtre*:
> Ma soeur, quelle voix nous appelle?
> UNE AUTRE
> J'en reconnais les agréables sons:
> C'est la reine.
>
> TOUTES DEUX
> Courons, mes soeurs, obéissons.
> La reine nous appelle:
> Allons, rangeons-nous auprès d'elle.
> TOUT LE CHOEUR, *entrant sur la scène par plusieurs endroits différents.*
> La reine nous appelle:
> Allons, rangeons-nous auprès d'elle.
>
> ELISE
> Ciel! quel nombreux essaim d'innocentes beautés
> S'offre à mes yeux en foule, et sort de tous côtés! (820)

This choral entry is set apart both visually and stylistically. On the one hand, the choreographed in-gathering imitates the perfect closure of the holy land and offers a visual antithesis to the exiles' dispersion. And on the other the choral form itself — singing as opposed to speech — creates a stylistic *écart* which figures a metaphysical distance: Esther's *détachement du monde au milieu du monde même.*

The end of the chorus brings out another aspect of the sanctuarial space. Esther sees a man approaching, whom she does not immediately recognize as her uncle. She challenges him, "Quel profane en ce lieu s'ose avancer vers nous?" The sanctuary is a forbidden place, dangerous to the heathen interloper. It thus becomes the symbolic pendant to the throne room, *lieu redoutable* where none can enter without the King's express leave:

> Hélas! ignorez-vous quelles sévères lois
> Aux timides mortels cachent ici les rois?
> Au fond de leur palais leur majesté terrible
> Affecte à leurs sujets de se rendre invisible;
> Et la mort est le prix de tout audacieux
> Qui, sans être appelé, se présente à leurs yeux,
> Si le roi dans l'instant, pour sauver le coupable,
> Ne lui donne à baiser son sceptre redoutable. (I.3.823)

The King, a god-like invisible presence, has the power to take or restore life. The end towards which Racine's apocalyptic vision tends is the co-location of throne and sanctuary, of temporal and spiritual power, in one place and in one Person: the new Jerusalem, ruled by Christ, the King descended. While this union cannot be accomplished in the play — Ahasuerus remains the enlightened but pagan king — it is symbolically prefigured when Esther asks the chorus to seek sanctuary by the throne: "Et vous, troupe jeune et timide, / Sans craindre ici les yeux d'une profane cour, / *A l'abri* de ce trône attendez mon retour" (II.8.841, emphasis mine).

At this point, the focus of the play shifts from concealment to revelation. On a literal level, the heroine finally discloses her true identity: "Esther, seigneur, eut un juif pour son père" (853). But revelation also enjoys its full religious meaning as the Truth unveiled. This symbolic theme becomes explicit in II.6, at approximately the midpoint of the play. Ahasuerus states in the prophetic language of the Bible: "*On verra* l'innocent *discerné* du coupable" (838). The chorus takes up and amplifies this idea at the end of the act: "Quand sera le voile arraché / Qui sur tout l'univers jette une nuit si sombre? / Dieu d'Israël, dissipe enfin cette ombre: / Jusqu'à quand seras-tu caché?" (II.7.842). These lines reveal a complex layering of biblical allusion. The repeated interrogatives *quand* and *jusqu'à quand* recall the syntactic pattern of Psalm 13: "How long, O Lord? Wilt thou forget me for ever? / How long wilt thou hide thy face from me?" God, in quasi-personal wrath against his people, refuses to look at them. Racine adds an allusion to the Second Epistle to the Corinthians: "To this day whenever Moses is read a veil lies over their minds; yes, but when a man turns to the Lord, the veil is removed" (3:15-16). In the New Testament passage, the concealment of God's face becomes a metaphor for the Old Testament read by non-Christian eyes: truth seen through a veil. This imposition of a figurative reading upon a concrete image recalls Augustin's injunction against taking Scripture literally or, as he puts it, "carnally." In reference to Psalm 13, he states, "they who, in a most carnal spirit, ascribe to God the form of a human body, may know that the turning away and turning again of His countenance is not like those motions of our own frame."[14] Racine's own version marks a further removal from the concrete. Both God and the creation are obscured; the face disappears, and the veil is generalized into a metaphysical darkness.

In terms of theater, this incursion of the metaphysical makes *Esther* very different from Racine's earlier plays. In a Greek-inspired tragedy like *Phèdre*, dramatic interest centers on recognition — the gradual acquiring of inner knowledge by the main characters. For this internal process of recognition, *Esther* substitutes the external mechanism of revelation: the *deus ex machina*, literally descending. This descent is accomplished through both natural and supernatural means. Racine begins by making full use of the well-made plot he found in the Book of Esther. Mordecai, the unseen power behind the throne, brings about Esther's marriage to Ahasuerus and then exhorts her to defend the Jews against Haman. The critical moment comes in II.4 when Esther reveals her identity and pleads for her people's safety. Before beginning her main speech, she calls on God, the unseen actor/spectator, to lend her eloquence: "O Dieu, confonds l'audace et l'imposture!" (853). She then recapitulates the main historic theme of the play, the Judeans' transgressions punished by exile, and concludes by praising Ahasuerus and accusing his advisor: "Un ministre ennemi de votre propre gloire" (854).

Esther's tirade, as a means of persuasion, is curiously lacking in *élan*. Though it received the approval of Voltaire, the speech, to modern ears, has a school-girlish stiffness. Esther nowhere manifests the

[14] *Exposition on the Book of Psalms* (Oxford: John Henry Parker, 1850) IV.278. Referred to in the text as *Homilies*.

eloquence of Chimène, for example, crying justice for her father, or, to restrict the comparison to Racine, the passion of Clytemnestra arguing for Iphigénie's life. Yet such as it is, it serves its purpose. It is as though in this situation of half-immanence, just *saying* the truth suffices. When Esther declares that Haman, not Mordecai, is the *perfide étranger* of Ahasuerus' dream, the King is seriously swayed. "J'étais donc le jouet ... Ciel, daigne m'éclairer" (856).

At this highly dramatic moment, Ahasuerus undramatically leaves the stage. His departure appears insufficiently motivated: "Un moment sans témoins cherchons à respirer, / Appelez Mardochée; il faut aussi l'entendre (*le roi s'éloigne*)." Ahasuerus' exit is founded on the biblical narrative, which Racine follows literally: "And the king rose from the feast in wrath and went into the palace garden" (Esther 7:1). Once again, Racine accommodates the biblical material to his own symbolic design. In the Bible, the King's departure is psychologically and dramatically convincing. In Racine's version, psychological and dramatic considerations are sacrificed to the underlying metaphysical imperative: Ahasuerus must exit because revelation, like murder, takes place *sans témoins*. As he departs, a young Israelite comments, "Vérité que j'implore, achève de descendre." This choral intervention underlines the external forms Ahasuerus' "enlightenment" will take: truth, invisible, will descend from the heavens into the wings.

At Ahasuerus' return, Haman's fate is sealed. In the biblical version, Haman is condemned for allegedly attempting to molest Esther: "and the King said: *Will he even assault the queen in my presence, in my own house*? As the word left the mouth of the King, they covered Haman's face" (in token of the sentence of death or as a sign of anger [Esther 7:8]). Racine borrows this pretext for Haman's execution — "Quoi? le traître sur vous porte ses mains hardies?" (857) — but the real cause of his downfall is more fundamental. The Ahasuerus who has returned to the stage is a changed man who now can discern the truth: "Ah! dans ses yeux confus je lis ses perfidies; / Et son trouble, appuyant la foi de votre discours, / De tous ses attentats me rappelle le cours." This speech confirms the chorus' assertion of III.3: "Un roi sage, ennemi du langage menteur / Ecarte d'un regard le perfide imposteur" (851). The subsequent entrance of Mordecai in III.7 completes Ahasuerus' enlightenment: "Mortel chéri du ciel, mon salut et ma joie, / Aux conseils des méchants ton roi n'est plus en proie: / Mes yeux sont dessillés, le crime est confondu" (858). The sight of Mordecai reinforces Ahasuerus' new vision because, resplendent in ministerial robes, he incarnates the union of spiritual and temporal power which Ahasuerus' "conversion" has mediated. Mordecai's new splendor reflects the Majesty which descended to transform the secular world.[15] But this descent, this moment of truth, remains unseen. To return to our earlier formulation, revelation only occurs "offstage": it is solitary, noncommunicable, and nonverbal. At the critical point, language fades; truth is unmediated by words, even spoken in innocence.

However, this is not the whole story. It is not enough that the source of evil be identified; for the pre-exilic order to be reestablished, for things to move back into their proper place, the evil must be expurgated completely. And, in *Esther*, as in *Phèdre*, *le mal vient de loin*, through the veins of the protagonists. We learn in scene 3 that Esther, as well as her companions, are Benjaminites: "Toi qui de Benjamin comme moi descendue." Through Benjamin, they trace their ancestry back to Jacob, chosen of God, later named Israel: "De l'antique Jacob jeune postérité." Esther prays to God:

> Mon père mille fois m'a dit dans mon enfance
> Qu'avec nous tu juras une sainte alliance
> Quand, pour te faire un peuple agréable à tes yeux,
> Il plut à ton amour de choisir nos aïeux. (I.4.824)

Haman, in contrast, is the *perfide étranger*. According to the additions to *Esther*, he is a Macedonian, an Idumean exile descended from the Amalekites. This people, archetypal enemies of the Jews, plays a notorious role in the Old Testament. When Joseph was fleeing Egypt, the forces of Amalek attacked him in the desert, incurring the wrath of God: "And the Lord said to Moses, 'Write this as a memorial in a book and recite it in the ears of Joshua, that I will utterly blot out the remembrance of Amalek from under heaven... The lord will have war with Amalek from generation to generation'" (Exodus 17:14, 16). Like the Philistines and Moabites, the Amalekites continue to be a traditional enemy of the Israelites. In Deuteronomy, when the laws were laid down, the Jews are again reminded to "blot out" the Amalekites "who did not fear God" (25:18). In the Book of Samuel, Saul massacres the Amalekites, taking only the King Agag alive (15:8-9).

[15] For a different point of view, see J. A. Nelson, "La Fonction de la connaissance dans *Esther*," *Nottingham French Studies* 18: 1-8.

In Racine's *Esther*, this past history is brought out much more explicitly than in the Old Testament version. In the Book of Esther, there is no mention of Haman's ancestral hatred and no explanation of why Mordecai will not bow to him (Esther 3:3-4). In Racine's play, on the other hand, the issue of Aman's ancestry is raised early on. Hydaspe asks Aman:

> Ce n'est donc pas, seigneur, le sang amalécite,
> Dont la voix à les perdre en secret vous excite?

Aman replies:

> Je sais que, descendu de ce sang malheureux,
> Une éternelle haine a dû m'armer contre eux;
> Qu'ils firent d'Amalec un indigne carnage;
> Que, jusqu'aux vils troupeau, tout éprouva leur rage;
> (II.1.832)

But he denies any racial motive to his action against the Jews:

> Mon âme, à la grandeur tout entière attachée,
> Des intérêts du sang est faiblement touchée,
> Mardochée est coupable; et que faut-il de plus? (833)

Because Mardochée would not bow down before him his pride orders that all the Jews be destroyed.

However, this is not the last we hear of Aman's fatal ancestry. In III.2, Aman admits he belongs to a *race maudite*: "J'ai chéri, j'ai cherché la malédiction" (847). For this reason his wife, Zarès, tries to warn him against entering into conflict with Mardochée, urging him to flee while there is yet time:

> Les malheurs sont souvent enchaînés l'un à l'autre,
> Et sa race fut toujours fatale à la vôtre ...
> Regagnez l'Hellespont et ces bords écartés
> Où vos aïeux errants jadis furent jetés,
> Lorsque des Juifs contre eux la vengeance allumée
> Chassa tout Amalec de la triste Idumée.
> Aux malices du sort enfin dérobez-vous.

Zarès uses the language of destiny (*malheurs*, *fatale*, *sort*) in speaking of this ancestral hatred. And in III.4, Esther reveals a similar reason for Mardochée's act of defiance:

> Plein d'une juste horreur pour un Amalécite,
> Il n'a devant Aman pu fléchir les genoux,

Ni lui rendre un honneur qu'il ne croit dû qu'à vous.
De là contre les Juifs et contre Mardochée
Cette haine, seigneur, sous d'autres noms cachée.
(855-56)

Thus, Aman's condemnation of the Jews has a deeper motive than he himself wishes to admit. This subtext, introduced by Racine, explains not only Aman's ferocity but Esther's as well, her refusal to grant Aman mercy: he is not only a threat to her people but represents their archetypal enemy. Thus, the somewhat child-like picture visible on the surface has profound underpinnings. On this level, *Esther* does not greatly differ from Racine's earlier tragedies; it comes out of a series — *La Thébaïde, Andromaque, Iphigénie, Phèdre* — in which hereditary conflicts end in violence.

The innocent children's choruses — to which we will return — do not neutralize the dark, bloody side of the story. On the contrary, Racine emphasizes the violent aspect of his work much more than the biblical story had done. In the Book of Esther, Haman is merely hanged; Racine, in contrast, gives us a sanguinary account of his death which looks forward to *Athalie*:

Seigneur, le traître est expiré,
Par le peuple en fureur à moitié déchiré
On traîne, on va donner en spectacle funeste
De son corps tout sanglant le misérable reste. (III.8.858)

Aman, one of the few remaining of his race (*déplorable reste*, II.1), is now reduced still further, to remains of remains.

The violence of Aman's end, of course, responds to the violence he planned to inflict on the Jews, as related in the girls' chorus of I.5:

Quel carnage de toutes parts!
On égorge à la fois les enfants, les vieillards,
Et la soeur, et le frère,
Et la fille, et la mère,
Le fils dans les bras de son père!
Que de corps entassés
Que de membres épars,
Privés de sépultures!
Grand Dieu! tes Saints sont la pâture
Des tigres et des léopards. (I.5.827)

This imagined holocaust perhaps justifies the manner of Aman's end; but the beginning of the final chorus, "Dieu fait triompher l'innocence," still rings strangely in contrast, unless one understands the necessary mechanism of sacrifice in the play. As in *Iphigénie*, the guilty victim is substituted for the innocent; Aman, like Eriphile, is a creature of darkness, rejected by God. And as in *Iphigénie*, there must be enough similarity between the innocent and guilty for the substitution to have validity. The Jews, like the Amalekites, are remainders: *de Jacob ... les restes* (I.3.822). Both are exiled, wandering peoples, both nearly exterminated, although one has received God's protection, the other his malediction.[16] Like the Child in *Athalie*, the characters in *Esther* are both innocent and sanguinary. Haman's destruction is an innocent act because it permits the Jews' salvation and the epiphany-like ending of the play.

While this epiphany cannot be revealed in speech, it can be celebrated. The final chorus of *Esther* accomplishes this celebration by a reversal of the initial metaphors of the play. Exile becomes return, the destruction of Jerusalem is answered in its rebuilding: "Quand verrai-je, ô Sion! relever tes remparts / Et de tes tours les magnifiques faîtes?" (I.2.821); "Relevez, relevez les superbes portiques / Du temple où notre Dieu se plaît d'être adoré" (III.9.861). Once again, Racine draws his imagery from Isaiah. "Put on your beautiful garments, O Jerusalem the holy city. Shake yourself from the dust, arise: O captive Jerusalem" (32:1-2). "Réjouis-toi, Sion, et sors de la poussière; / Quitte les vêtements de ta captivité, / Et reprends ta splendeur première" (860). Throughout this passage, the reversal of the exile cycle is emphasized by the use of the prefix *r(e)*: "*re*prends ta splendeur première; *Re*passez les monts et les mers; *Ra*ssemblez-vous des bouts de l'univers" (repeated); "je *re*verrai ces campagnes si chères; "*Re*levez, *re*levez les superbes portiques."

This *sème* of return leads finally to the culminating point of Racine's apocalyptic vision, "Dieu descend et revient habiter parmi nous." This line recalls Psalm 90, "Lord, thou hast been our dwelling place in all generations... Return, O Lord! How long?" (13). But it also introduces into the Old Testament context the neoplatonic tonalities of John 1:4: "And the Word became flesh and dwelt among us." The return of God will signal the liberation from temporal bonds. For the imperative of the Psalm and John's historic past, Racine substitutes

[16] According to a legendary tradition, the Malekites were descended from Esau, Jacob's ill-favored brother whose offering was spurned by his father. Thus, the play contains a hidden subtext of *frères ennemis*.

the timeless present of prophecy: *Dieu revient*, he *is* coming back. And this divine promise is underscored by a return to the animism of the first chorus. Once again, earth and skies are alive to God's potency: "Terre, frémis d'allégresse et de crainte, / Et vous, sous sa majesté sainte, / Cieux, abaissez-vous!" (861). This last image, of a baroque audacity, is drawn from Psalm 18:9: "He bowed the heavens and came down." But it also recalls the apocalyptic vision of the New Jerusalem, already present in Jewish mystic texts dating from as early as the first century C.E. According to Yehuda Shamir, "there were Jewish traditions that must have fed the essentially Jewish apocalyptic vision of St. John the Divine" (52): "Then I saw a new heaven and a new earth... And I saw the holy city, new Jerusalem, coming down out of heaven from God, prepared as a bride adorned for her husband... And night shall be no more; they need no light of lamp or sun, for the Lord God will be their light, and they shall reign for ever and ever" (Revelation 21-22). Racine's play ends with a lyrical invocation to praise God "forever and ever": "Au-delà des temps et des âges, / Au-delà de l'éternité!" In this hyperbolic finale, it is no longer a question of time's reversal, but of its abolition.

While he was probably unaware of any affinity with Jewish mysticism, Racine was likely to have read Augustine. The latter comments on the translation of Psalm 90:3, "from age to age thou art," "It would have been better, from everlasting to everlasting. For God, who is before the ages, exists not from a certain age... But [the translator] very rightly does not say thou wast from ages, and unto ages thou shalt be: but puts the verb in the present, intimating that the substance of God is altogether immutable... Behold then the eternity that is our refuge, that we may fly thither from the mutability of time" (*Homilies* IV.272). The exile's final destination is revealed as a realm beyond time, *au-delà de l'éternité*, in the sense that the very concepts of time and eternity will no longer have meaning or utility. "It is not, He was, and shall be, but only is." According to the Ferguson article cited above, language itself is a form of exile, because it shares the spatial and temporal limitations of the earthly state. I would argue that for Augustine, as for Racine, the road to exile can also be the road to return. And the figurative language of the Bible, renewed by Racine, is a signpost along that road.

But Racine, as a writer, has found another return: *Esther* closes the cycle opened by *Andromaque*, in which reconciliation was impossible and the return of the exiles an unrealizable dream. The destruction of Troy, the lamentations of *Andromaque la désolée*, which so touched

Racine in the *Iliad*[17] and the *Trojan Women*, have been absorbed and transmuted into the triumph of Esther and the rebirth of the new Jerusalem. And by this alchemy of poetry, Troy is reborn as well. Clearly, Racine does not end his career with the non-ocular vision proposed by Richard Barnett. On the other hand, the knowledge finally acquired does not follow the verifiable scientific model outlined by Timothy Reiss. As Sigmund Freud, father of the "science" of psychiatry, would have appreciated, Racine's is a knowledge guarded by poets.[18]

[17] In the margin of the *Iliad* VI.390, Racine had written "paroles divines d'Andromaque" (II.114).

[18] "If you want to know more about femininity, enquire from your own experiences of life, or turn to the poets, or wait until science can give you deeper and more coherent information" ("Femininity," *Complete Works of Sigmund Freud*, ed. James Strachery [London: Hogarth, 1964] XXII.135).

4. Pascal and the Discourse of the Inexpressible

This chapter deals, alternatively or simultaneously, with rhetoric, reading, and theology. For Pascal, though a Christian apologist, is not so far from the dramatic world of Corneille and Racine. Like Racine, he strives to express, or at least allude to, incomprehensible divine truths. Like Corneille, he perceives human discourse as multifaceted and dialectic, reflecting the viewpoints it aims to convey. On yet another level, sacred discourse itself eschews rhetoric in an effort to reach the transcendent. All these aspects of Pascal's work are related to reading. In a first section, I will discuss the rhetoric of the Pascalian apologist attempting to present contradictory truths to the reader. The second part treats Augustine's and Pascal's methods of reading Scripture, again emphasizing the paradoxical reading of the unreadable.

> Toutes choses changent et se succèdent.
> Vous vous trompez, il y a ... (*Pensées* L26, B227)

In contemplating his apologetic venture, Pascal might well have said: *scribo, quia impossibile*. For the fundamental project of the *Pensées* is an epistemological paradox. Through verbal persuasion, Pascal wishes to convince the unbeliever of truths which are not only unprovable, but inexpressible in words. For the Augustinian Pascal, "... l'homme est déchu d'un état de gloire et de communication avec Dieu en un état de tristesse, de pénitence et d'éloignement de Dieu"[1] (L281,

[1] Quotations from the *Pensées* are based on the Lafuma edition in Pascal, *Oeuvres complètes* (Paris: Seuil, 1963). Translations are mine. Further references, to both the

B613). God is *incommunicado*: unspeaking, unspeakable, infinitely removed from human ken. What can Pascal presume to say when God Himself is silent?

I will approach this question through an analysis of human and divine discourse in the *Pensées*. I intend to show that the *Pensées* do not resolve the paradox of communicating the incommunicable, but rather assimilate it into their structure. Pascal's *Pensées* are governed by a rhetoric of discontinuity. Discontinuity because man is a creature of change and caprice, of fleeting passions: *l'éloquence continue ennuie* (L771, B355). But discontinuity as well because in the classical view, man's understanding is radically finite. The truth we perceive is determined by our point of view. As Timothy Reiss says of Galileo: "For him discourse represents not the object itself but the distance between the object and the mind *per*ceiving it, and then *con*ceiving it" (*Science, Language* 7). For Pascal, as for Galileo, knowledge is a function of perspective: "les choses sont vraies ou fausses selon la face par où on les regarde" (L539, B99). This perspective-bound epistemology verges on relativism: "Le langage est pareil de tous côtés. Il faut avoir un point fixe pour en juger. Le port juge ceux qui sont dans un vaisseau, mais où prendrons-nous un port dans la morale?" (L697, B383). However, Pascal stops short of total skepticism: "naturellement l'homme ne peut tout voir, et ... naturellement il ne se peut tromper dans le côté qu'il envisage; comme les appréhensions des sens sont toujours vraies" (L701, B9). In answer to the Skeptic's universal error, Pascal proposes a universe of fragmentary truths — shards of belief.

This epistemology of fragmentation implies its own rhetorical strategy: "Quand on veut reprendre avec utilité, et montrer à un autre qu'il se trompe, il faut observer par quel côté il envisage la chose, car elle est vraie ordinairement de ce côté-là" (L701, B9). The result of this strategy is a prismatic shattering of point of view: the narrator speaks in all voices but the familiar *tu* and (alas) the feminine. "Otez leur divertissement, vous les verrez se sécher d'ennui, ils sentent alors leur néant sans le connaître; car c'est bien malheureux que d'être dans une tristesse insupportable, aussitôt qu'on est réduit à se considérer, et à n'en être point diverti" (L36, B164). In this passage the narrator first establishes a bond with his discerning reader (*vous*) in opposition

Lafuma and Brunschvicg editions, will appear in the text in abbreviation: i.e., L418, B233. For an accessible English translation, see Pascal, *Pensées*, tr. A. J. Krailsheimer (Baltimore: Penguin, 1966).

to the unenlightened *ils*, then eliminates this distinction by generalizing his remarks to all men: *vous* and *ils* yield to *on*. In another passage, *ils* takes on the denotation of *les incrédules*: "Qu'ils aprennent au moins quelle est la religion qu'ils combattent, avant de la combattre" (L427, B194). Again, *ils* can designate all mankind: "Tous les hommes recherchent d'être heureux; cela est sans exception; quelques différents moyens qu'ils y emploient, ils tendent tous à ce but" (L148, B425). These shifts in denotation reflect the rhetorical strategy of divide and conquer: "Plaindre les athées qui cherchent, car ne sont-ils pas assez malheureux? Invectiver contre ceux qui en font vanité" (L156, B190).

The most protean person in the *Pensées*, however, is the first. Pascal's supposedly detestable *moi* enjoys not just one identity, but several. We can distinguish the *moi pyrrhonien*: "J'ai vu tous les pays et hommes changeants; et ainsi, après bien des changements de jugement touchant la véritable justice, j'ai connu que notre nature n'était qu'un continuel changement et je n'ai plus changé depuis" (L520, B375). There is also the *moi qui cherche*: "... considérant combien il y a plus d'apparence qu'il y a autre chose que ce que je vois, j'ai recherché si ce Dieu n'aurait point laissé quelque marque de soi" (L198, B693). There is also a preacher-*moi* who at times replaces the third-person narrator: "Je ne puis avoir que de la compassion pour ceux qui gémissent sincèrement dans ce doute ..." (L427, B194). And so on; the examples are legion. This polyphonic narration conveys stylistically the epistemological premise of finiteness: the only "omniscient narrator" is God Himself.

Pascal also displaces point of view in a physical sense. In the *deux infinis* text (*disproportion de l'homme*), by telescoping time and space, he forces the reader to contemplate the world from two opposing perspectives at once: "... qui n'admirera que notre corps, qui tantôt n'était pas perceptible dans l'univers, imperceptible lui-même dans le sein du tout, soit à présent un colosse, un monde, ou plutôt un tout, à l'égard du néant où l'on ne peut arriver?" (L199, B72). This shift in visual perspective metaphorically enacts the dispersion of our moral vision: "La nature de l'homme se considère en deux manières: l'une selon sa fin, et alors il est grand et incomparable; l'autre selon la multitude ... et alors l'homme est abject et vil" (L127, B415). What we see depends precisely on where we stand: *verité au-deçà des Pyrénées, erreur au-delà* (L60, B294).

This contextual certainty is reinforced by two complementary verbal structures, hyperbole and negation. Through hyperbole, an assertion expands to fill its contextual space: there is no room left for error. "Infiniment éloigné de comprendre les extrêmes, la fin des choses et leur principe sont pour lui invinciblement cachés dans un secret impénétrable. ... Bornés en tout genre, cet état qui tient le milieu entre deux extrêmes se trouve en toutes nos puissances" (L199, B72). Hyperbole turns the middle ground into an extremity. Negative constructions, on the other hand, restrict the rhetorical field to the context in question. The structure *rien ne ... que* occurs particularly often: "*Rien n*'est si important à l'homme *que* son état; *rien ne* lui est si redoutable *que* l'éternité. ... *Rien n*'accuse davantage une extrême faiblesse d'esprit *que* de ne pas connaître quel est le malheur d'un homme sans Dieu; *rien ne* marque davantage une mauvaise disposition du coeur *que* de ne pas souhaiter la vérité des promesses éternelles" (L427, B194). The techniques of hyperbole and negation, of rhetorical expansion and contraction, often work together in the same sentence: "Je regarde de toutes parts, et je ne vois partout qu'obscurité" (L429, B229). Through this combination of techniques, the contextual foreground is illuminated, leaving all else in darkness.

The other side of total certainty-within-context is total opposition between contexts. Pascal is perhaps the most contrary of all writers, and analyses of his inconsistencies have filled many books. I will limit myself here to a brief discussion of the Pascalian concept of *nature*. What is the nature of man? "La nature de l'homme est toute nature, *omne animal*" (L630, B94). One animal nature. Then again, "La coûtume est une second nature, qui détruit la première" (L126, B93). Now we have two natures: but which two? "Imagination: cette superbe puissance, ennemie de la raison, qui se plaît à la contrôler et à la dominer ... a établi dans l'homme une seconde nature" (L44, B82). "La concupiscence nous est devenue naturelle, et a fait notre seconde nature. Ainsi, il y a deux natures en nous: l'une bonne, l'autre mauvaise" (L616, B660). "Instinct et raison, marques de deux natures" (L112, B344).

I will not attempt to reconcile these contradictory definitions: *au contraire*. For Pascal himself places unresolved contradiction at the heart of his discourse: "Les deux raisons contraires. Il faut commencer par là: sans cela, on n'entend rien, et tout est hérétique: et même, à la fin de chaque vérité, il faut ajouter qu'on se souvient de la vérité opposée" (L576, B576). Not one apparent truth, but two opposing truths, truth and anti-truth. Why this deliberate courting of contradiction? On one level, contradiction, like hyperbole, is a persuasive technique which evokes certain reactions in the reader. While hyperbole transmits certitude, contradiction provokes confusion and fatigue: "Quelque parti qu'il prenne, je ne l'y laisserai point en repos ..." (L449,

B556). This fatiguing mental exercise, by wearing out the brain, may help break down the unbeliever's rational resistance to conversion. However, its rhetorical efficacy alone does not account for the pervasiveness of contradiction in the *Pensées*. As we have seen, the discourse of the *Pensées* is sinuous and multi-faceted. Its structure, if one can use the term at all, is disjointed not by biographical accident, but in its very essence. Pascal's thought resists synthesis because each passage creates its own context and thereby its own "truth," which supersedes previous truths, only to be superseded in its turn. In our intellectual *misère*, *Les Pensées* (pl.) cannot be reduced to *la pensée* (sing.).

Thus far we have considered the *Pensées* as human discourse, *selon les lumières naturelles* (L418, B233). In this natural light, the text emerges as a cluster of circumscribed, self-limiting truths. However, this description cannot apply to divine discourse. Before considering Pascal's treatment of this discourse, let us see how his master Augustine describes it.

> ... he heard things that cannot be told,
> which man may not utter. (2 Corinthians 12:4)

I will begin this discussion with a parable. There was once a young student of rhetoric, who lived wholly given over to the pleasures of love and eloquence. One day, while pursuing his studies, he came upon a book which changed his life. This book, Cicero's *Hortentius*, so inflamed his heart with the love of wisdom (philosophy) that he began reading the Holy Scriptures. However, he did not find in the Scriptures what he was seeking, because their style put him off: "... they seemed to me far unworthy to be compared to the stateliness of the Ciceronian eloquence. For my swelling pride soared above the temper of their style, nor was my sharp wit able to pierce into their sense."[2] As a result, the student of rhetoric (and subsequent rhetorician) spent ten years wandering amid false doctrines, first "ensnared by the Manichees," then bemused by astrology, before he finally found true wisdom in the true (Catholic) faith.

As you will have surmised, the hero of this parable is Augustine, as he describes himself in the *Confessions*. I have returned to Augustine

[2] Augustine, *Confessions*, tr. William Watts, Loeb Classical Library (London: Heinemann; New York: Macmillan, 1912) III.v.113. Despite its occasional awkwardnesses and inaccuracies, I prefer this old translation because it remains close to Augustine's Latin and best conveys its poetic quality. A more modern, colloquial translation is that of R. S. Pine-Coffin (Baltimore: Penguin, 1961).

and the *Confessions* because they dramatize almost to the point of allegory the paradoxical relation uniting rhetoric to religious truth. The reading of rhetorical works, which here include profane literature in general — Greek and Latin poets — awakened Augustine's spiritual faculty. But the habit of such reading made sacred texts incomprehensible to him. However, the impenetrability of sacred discourse is not just a matter of taste or habit. Augustine is raising here, in a broad and essentially modern sense, the question of reading. He says there is something basic to the Scriptures, to the reader, or to both, which prevents proper reading from taking place. What causes this unreadability, and how can it be cured? These are questions which Augustine addresses explicitly in *De Doctrina christiana* [*Of Christian Instruction*], a work roughly contemporaneous to the *Confessions*.[3] In the preface to *De Doctrina*, Augustine announces his aim: to teach rules for the interpretation of Scripture. He then assimilates this act of interpretation to the act of reading: "... he who explains to listeners what he understands in the Scriptures... is like a reader who pronounces the words he knows, but he who teaches how the Scriptures are to be understood is like a teacher who advises how the words are to be read."[4] Augustine thus defines his role not as a reader, but as a teacher of reading.

On the other hand, my interpretive role in this chapter, as in the book as a whole, is more akin to reading than to teaching. I will propose readings of two different texts, each of which calls forth a somewhat different method. The first reading is of Augustine's rules for reading the Scriptures in *De Doctrina*. The second, undertaken in the light of the first, deals with Pascal's biblical exegesis in the *Pensées*. Of course, Pascal's Augustinian heritage in theology is common ground among scholars, but his debt to Augustine in the domain of biblical interpretation is less well known.[5] While it may be true of Pascal,

[3] The *Confessions* date from approximately 397-401 C.E., the first three books of *De Doctrina* from 396. The fourth book, which deals more with rhetoric than with interpretation of Scripture, was written in 427. For a critical edition of Book IV, see *De Doctrina christiana*, Liber IV, ed. Sister Thérèse Sullivan (Washington: Catholic University of America, 1930).

[4] *On Christian Doctrine*, tr. D. W. Robertson, Jr. (Indianapolis, New York: Bobbs-Merrill, 1956) Prologue 9, 7. Further references to this work will appear in the text. The original Latin text is found in *Sancti Avreli Augustini Opera*, Sect. V, Pars VI (Vienna: Hoelder-Pichler-Tempsky, 1963. Corpus Scriptorum Ecclesiasticorum Latinorum, LXXX).

[5] In *Pascal et St-Augustin* (Paris: Colin, 1970) 382-424, Philippe Sellier gives an excellent analysis of the meaning of the Scriptures in both authors. However, he is

as Jan Miel has written, that "his emphasis on linguistic analysis is virtually unique in theological writing before the twentieth century" (191), it is also true that Augustine came first. Thus, the views of Augustine and Pascal on biblical discourse make an interesting chapter in three ahistorical histories: those of theology, of reading, and of language.

As I have already suggested, for Augustine the problems we encounter in reading Scripture are more than rhetorical; they are also theological. On a theological level, the obstacles to our understanding of Scripture arise from two sources: man and God. Human nature, and above all the besetting sin of pride, blind us to religious truth. As Augustine states in the passage from the *Confessions* already quoted: "my swelling pride soared above the temper [moderation] of their style, nor was my sharp wit able to pierce into their sense." "Sharp wit" is pejorative here, an intellectual variant of "swelling pride." Until he was able to humble himself, to "stoop his neck to its coming," Augustine understood nothing of religious language or truth.

If human nature is one obstacle to our reading of Scripture, God's nature is another. At the beginning of *De Doctrina*, Augustine states that there is an interdiction on direct contact with the divine. Alluding to 2 Corinthians (see above, p. 107), he admonished the reader: "We should not tempt Him in whom we have believed, lest... we should be unwilling to go to church to hear and learn the Gospels, or to read a book, or to hear a man reading or teaching, but expect to be 'caught up to the third heaven,' as the Apostle says, 'whether in the body or out of the body,' and there hear 'secret words that man may not repeat,' or there see Our Lord Jesus Christ and hear the gospel from Him rather than from men" (Prologue 5, 5). According to Augustine, the passage from Corinthians records the breaking of two interdictions. The first is on hearing "secret words": in Latin *ineffabila verba*, words which cannot be uttered. Divine discourse, the true Name of God, are not fit for human ears. The second interdiction is against bypassing the human intermediary. Trying to communicate directly with God is, for Augustine, a dangerous temptation of pride. Nevertheless, he gives a relatively optimistic reason for this need of a human mediator: "And all of these things... might have been done by an angel, but the condition of man would be lowered if God had not wished to have men supply His word to men" (Prologue 6, 5). God honors

more interested in the theology of language than the language of theology, and, perhaps for this reason, deals relatively little with *De Doctrina*.

human beings by giving them a participatory role as ministers of His word.

In the context of *De Doctrina*, the men who "supply His word" (*verbum suum ministrare*) are the divinely inspired authors of the Scriptures. Since we cannot rise to the third heaven or speak with angels, we are thrown back on sacred texts. And since sacred texts speak of sacred mysteries, they must of necessity also be mysterious. Hence, the obscurity of Holy Scripture is an essential element of its sacredness. But that is not all. For Augustine, rhetorician turned theologican, the obscurity of the Scriptures is also inseparable from their special eloquence: "But behold, I espy something in them not revealed to the proud, not discovered unto children, humble in style, sublime in operation, and wholly veiled over in mysteries" (*Confessions* III.v.113). Scriptural mystery plays a complex rhetorical role for Augustine. On the one hand, obscurity is an attention-getting device: reading a difficult text exercises our faculties of concentration and helps alert us to the message of God. On the other hand, the mystery of Sacred texts is esthetically pleasing in itself: in commenting on the verse from the Song of Songs, "Thy teeth are as flocks of sheep that are shorn, which come up from the washing, all with twins, and there is none barren among them" (4:2), Augustine asks: "Does one learn anything else besides that which he learns when he hears the same thought expressed in plain words without this similitude? Nevertheless, in a strange way, I contemplate the saints more pleasantly when I envisage them as the teeth of the Church cutting off men from their errors and transferring them to her body after their hardness has been softened as if by being bitten and chewed" (*De Doctrina* II.vi.7.37). Why figurative language is pleasanter than plain language is an esthetic mystery he does not attempt to solve.

This mysterious sacred rhetoric, which Augustine was unable to appreciate on first reading, he now aspires to interpret for others or, more precisely, to teach others to interpret for themselves. In Augustine's method of interpretation, the key concepts are the sign and figure. He gives this definition of the sign: "A thing which causes us to think of something beyond the impression the thing itself makes upon the senses" (*De Doctrina* II.i.1.34). Unlike Port-Royal and Saussurian signs, Augustinian signs do not contain within themselves the idea which they seek to represent (*le signifié*, in Saussure's terms). Instead, they are arrows pointing, as Augustine says, to something beyond or something else (*aliud aliquid*). In an attempt to distinguish between literary and nonliterary signs, critics of our time have offered formulas close to Augustine's. According to Michael Riffaterre, for example, "literature, by saying something, says something else."[6] Thus, literary discourse becomes "divinized" in relation to "normal" discourse: the latter is merely literal and mimetic, the former symbolic and "semiotic." A search for the Augustinian "metaphysics" behind these current literary models might yield most interesting results; but this subject lies beyond the scope of our present inquiry.

To return to the strictly theological implications of Augustine's semiotics, they are obvious and important. Since God is unspeakable, His name (*Deus*) is not a true Name but rather a sign of the Augustinian type, whose function is to indicate Something Else (*De Doctrina* I.vi.6.11). In Augustine's words, the true function of signs is "to raise the eye of the mind above things that are corporal and created to drink in eternal light" (III.v.9.84). The neo-Platonism of this statement is self-evident; and it is the content-free nature of Augustinian signs that allows their Platonic light to shine through.

Significant as signs are in Augustine, it is with his discussion of figures that we arrive at the heart of his interpretive scheme. Although he sometimes uses the term "figure" in its rhetorical sense, saying for example that the Bible contains standard rhetorical tropes and figures, the importance of the figure for Augustine lies elsewhere. What particularizes sacred discourse, in fact, is a special function of figures. In the context of the Scriptures, figurative locutions "obscure the sense, or make an allegory or an enigma" (III.xi.17.90). People misread the Bible because they take these figurative passages literally. And they make this mistake because they are human, giving the word "human" all its theological weight: "For when that which is said figuratively is taken as though it were literal, it is understood *carnally*" (III.v.9.84, emphasis mine). Again, Augustine infuses linguistic analysis with spiritual meaning. People, housed in flesh, tend to see things carnally: "For the sense of our flesh is slow, even because it is the sense of our flesh; and itself its own measure (*ipse est modus eius*)" (*Confessions* IV.x.175).

Another way Augustine conveys man's spiritual bondage is to say "he is a slave to a sign" (*sub signum servit*; *De Doctrina* III.ix.13.86).

[6] *Semiotics of Poetry* (Bloomington: Indiana University Press, 1978) 17. Cf. also J. Brody's discussion of literary language in "From Teeth to Text in *De l'expérience*: A Philological Reading," *Esprit Créateur* 20.1 (Spring 1980) 9.

Augustine elaborates: "He is a slave who uses or worships a significant thing without knowing what it signifies." Thus, reading Scripture as a literal story is the same kind of enslavement as worshipping idols or following the mere outward practices of religion. The expression *sub signum servit*, serving under a sign, conveys an idea not only of slavery but almost of physical oppression under the weight of literal (carnal) meanings. But since humans are spirit as well as flesh, they have the capacity to free themselves from linguistic bondage, to distinguish literal from figurative discourse, appearance from truth. In other words, they can learn how to read.

Augustine's basic rule for reading appears simple, at least in theory: "what is read would be subjected to diligent scrutiny until an interpretation contributing to the reign of charity is produced" (III.xv.23.93). Everything in the Scriptures points toward this reign of charity as an ultimate end, and whatever cannot be made to render up this meaning literally must be taken "figuratively and prophetically" (III.xii.20.91). While he who takes a sign literally is in bondage, "He who uses or venerates a useful sign divinely instituted whose signifying force he understands does not venerate what he sees and what passes away but rather than to which all such things are to be referred" (III.ix.13.86-87). As this passage shows, Augustine's distinctions between sign, thing, and figure ultimately break down, because in the end all things are signs which figure and *pre*figure God.

To the reader acquainted with Pascal, Augustine's concept of the figure will have struck a familiar note. For both authors, the figure is a means for making the transition from human to divine truth. We live in the world among circumscribed, self-limiting truths; but Truth on a transcendent plane is One, not many. This unicity of meaning stems from God's nature as an infinite being: "L'unité jointe à l'infini ne l'augmente de rien, non plus qu'un pied à une mesure infinie" (L418, B233). But man, a finite creature, cannot comprehend the infinite, nor can a temporal being experience timelessness. "La dernière fin est ce qui donne le nom aux choses" (L502, B571), and this final end, the secret Name, we will not hear until the end of time ("on ne l'entendra qu'à la fin des temps" [L501, B659]).

And yet, across these apparently impassable barriers of time and space, God has communicated with us. Pascal says the history of the Church ought properly to be called the history of truth, of God's messages to humanity (L776, B858). The scriptural figure is one means of conveying these messages. Pascal conceives of the figure as operating metaphorically on several levels. Its duality matches the division of man into spirit and flesh, reason and instinct. The figure also represents the nature and function of the Bible: mixed human/divine discourse, mediating between man and God. Finally, biblical figures prefigure Christ, the figure incarnate, the Word made flesh who will mediate man's salvation.

Rhetorical intent also plays an important part in Pascal's theory of the figure. At times, he seems to portray God as a divine orator, deliberately framing his message to suit his audience: "Thus, in order to satisfy our curiosity, which seeks variety, God varies the sole precept of charity by such variety as ever leads us to the one thing necessary. For one thing alone is necessary, but we love variety; and God satisfies both by this kind of variety which leads to the one thing necessary" (L270, B670). By its repetitiveness and circularity, its very tautology, Pascal's writing conveys the monotony of divine discourse which, like the single note of the last trumpet, will awaken us at the end of time. Since people are not ready to hear this divine discourse in its pure monotonous form, its monotony must be clothed in variety — in figures.

Thus far, Pascal's concept of the figure does not appear to differ much from Augustine's, but divergence between Pascalian and Augustinian figures begins on a theological level. After Augustine, Pascal asks himself why the signs of divine presence in the world are so enigmatic. The answers he offers seem familiar: people are weak, God mysterious. But there is a difference in emphasis great enough to constitute a qualitative difference. For Pascal, the mystery of religious discourse is not merely a consequence of the disparity between divine and human natures, but a fact of central theological importance. Paradoxically, mystery reveals God's intentions: "Dieu s'est voulu cacher" (L242, B585). This notion of the hidden God, popularized by Lucien Goldmann,[7] runs through the *Pensées*. It also forms the subject of a letter to Mlle de Roannez which Pascal wrote at roughly the same time (October 1656). Since the letter is extremely illuminating, and hardly known except to Pascal specialists, I will quote from it at some length.

"If God discovered himself continually to men, there would be no merit in believing in him; and if he never discovered himself, there would be little faith. But he conceals himself ordinarily and discloses

[7] *Le Dieu caché* (Paris: Gallimard, 1955). In my view, Goldmann concentrates too much on God's absence rather than on his concealment. See below, note 12.

himself rarely..."[8] How does God conceal himself, according to Pascal? First, "sous le voile de la nature." As he points out in the *Pensées*, there is no use trying to prove the existence of God by pointing to the moon and stars. You will not convince anyone who is not convinced already, because He has hidden Himself too well. And He concealed Himself even better through the Incarnation: when God took on human form as Christ, even fewer people recognized Him than before. Pascal puts it in his characteristically paradoxical style: "He was much more recognizable when he was invisible" (letter to Mlle de Roannez 348).

Third, God conceals himself in the sacrament of the Eucharist:

> ... when he wished to fulfil the promise that he made to his apostles to remain with men until his final coming, he chose to remain in the strangest and most obscure secret of all, which are the species of the Eucharist. It is this sacrament that St. John calls in the Apocalypse *a concealed manner*; and I believe that Isaiah saw it in that state, when he said in the spirit of prophecy: *Truly thou art a God concealed*. This is the last secrecy wherein he can be. The veil of nature that covers God has been penetrated by some of the unbelieving who, as St. Paul says, have recognized an invisible God in visible nature. Heretical Christians have recognized him through his humanity and adored Jesus Christ God and man. But to recognize him under the species of bread is peculiar to Catholics alone: none but us are thus enlightened by God.

In this context, species (*espèces* in French) has a "specific" theological meaning: it refers to the bread and wine in the sacrament of communion, after transsubstantiation has taken place.[9] This definition revives the etymological meaning of the word: *species* in Latin means a sight or outward form. What we actually see when the sacrament is administered are only appearances of bread and wine which disguise the mystery of Christ's transformation.[10]

Finally, Pascal arrives at sacred discourse itself: "We may add to these considerations the secrecy of the spirit of God concealed still

[8] Translation from Pascal, *Thoughts and Minor Works*, Harvard Classics 48 (New York: Collier, 1938) 348-49. The French original is found in Pascal, *Oeuvres* 267.

[9] The source for this definition is Littré, *Dictionnaire de la langue française* (Paris: Hachette, 1881).

[10] The Eucharist was a highly debated subject from the Middle Ages on. This debate surfaces in the seventeenth century in a late (1683) addition to the Port-Royal *Logique*, which has been commented on extensively by Louis Marin: *Critique du discours* (Paris: Minuit, 1975).

in the Scripture. For there are two perfect senses, the literal and the mystical; and the Jews, stopping at the one, do not even think there is another...." Clearly, the four "species" of concealment discussed in this letter are viewed by Pascal as analogous, if not identical. In each case, the spiritual is enveloped in the physical: God is hidden in nature, then incarnate in man, then present in the Host, then finally concealed in the letter of the Scripture. Why does God conceal Himself in these myriad ways? Pascal's answer is implied at the beginning of his letter; "If God discovered Himself continually to man, there would be no merit in believing in Him." As Pascal will make clear in the *Pensées*, God's concealment is related to the Augustinian doctrines of predestination and election. God does not reveal Himself to everyone because not everyone is to be saved.

Pascal's doctrine of the elect clearly manifests itself in his theory of figures.[11] For him, the figurative language of the Bible has a peculiar theological function: to mislead the unworthy. "On n'entend rien aux ouvrages de Dieu si on ne prend pour principe qu'il a voulu aveugler les uns et eclaircir les autres" (L232, B566). In a long section entitled *loi figurative*, Pascal elaborates this theory of elective obscurity. For example, the Jews did not recognize the Messiah because prophecies had led them to expect an earthly king. Why did God cause Christ to be predicted in this misleading fashion? "pour rendre le Messie connaissable aux bons et méconnaissable aux méchants" (L255, B758).[12] The "carnal" Jews (Pascal again uses Augustine's terms) take the prophecies literally, and the fact that they take them literally proves that they do not deserve to take them figuratively.

Despite, or perhaps because of, the Augustinian tenor of his thought, Pascal's view of the Scriptures differs significantly from his master's.

[11] According to Sellier, the connection between predestination and biblical figures is already present in Augustine (Sellier 394). However, it is found in a small number of texts only, and does not dominate Augustine's exegetic approach as it does Pascal's. M. Marrou, as quoted by Sellier, puts the position well: "Dans quelques textes, j'entrevois de façon fugitive l'idée pascalienne de l'obscurité voulue par Dieu pour aveugler les uns et éclairer les autres. ... L'idée est d'ailleurs chez Pascal plus augustinienne (au sens janséniste) que chez Augustin lui-même ou sa valeur est plutôt morale et n'est pas liée à la hantise de la prédestination" (*Saint Augustin et la fin de la culture antique* [Paris: de Boccard, 1938] 487; quoted in Sellier 392).

[12] Pascal's word choice reflects a nuance hard to convey in English: Christ is not *inconnaissable* (unrecognizable) but *méconnaissable* (difficult to recognize, heavily disguised). Pascal's notion of the hidden god is a complex and dialectical one, in which absence can be more revealing than presence.

For Augustine, reading Scripture is an act that changes the reader, that can in fact lead to the most fundamental kind of change — conversion. Pascal must share this view of reading to some extent, or he would despair of undertaking an Apology at all. And yet, the Scriptures for Pascal are less a tool for conversion than a screen or filter. His own image is stronger; the literal sense of the Bible is a rat-trap (*une ratière*) which catches the wicked, letting the just escape (L827, B673). Or, to put the matter in pedagogical terms, the difference between Augustine's and Pascal's reading of Scripture is the difference between teaching and testing. Augustine's God teaches; Pascal's God tests.

However, Pascal again rejoins Augustine at a later (or higher) point. Pascal's linguistic concepts form an interlocking hierarchy, rising from the human to the divine. Human discourse is wholly rhetorical, in aim as in essence. Sacred discourse shares with the human its rhetorical intentionality, but replaces multiple probabilities with a single certainty. Within this hierarchy, the relation between human and biblical discourse is represented by the figure, through which diversity signifies oneness, flesh signifies spirit. At these upper limits, Pascal's notion of figures reintegrates Augustinian neo-Platonism. Bereft of its own signified, the visible world becomes merely a signifier, a metaphorical reflection of the invisible: "Car la nature est une image de la grâce" (L503, B675). But even here, the ascent is not over: "Et même la grâce n'est que la figure de la gloire. Car elle n'est pas la dernière fin" (L275, B643).

And what of this final end? Since we cannot ascend to the third heaven and speak with God, we can have no real notion of "pure" divine discourse. But Pascal's (and Augustine's) neo-Platonism give us a clue to its possible nature. For theirs is neo-Platonism of a special sort: objects on earth, instead of reflecting their respective archetypes in heaven, all share one single referent ("illud potius quo talia cuncta referenda sunt"; *De Doctrina* III.ix.13). Although we cannot imagine such a discourse, divine discourse must be one in which all distinctions are abolished. "Différence entre le diner et le souper. En Dieu la parole ne diffère pas de l'intention, car il est véritable; ni la parole de l'effet, car il est puissant; ni les moyens de l'effet, car il est sage" (L968, B654). As we know from reading Derrida,[13] the verb *différer* in French means both "to differ" and "to defer"; thus, God's

[13] *L'Ecriture et la différence* (Paris: Seuil, 1967), *De la grammatologie* (Paris: Minuit, 1967).

will abolishes both conceptual and temporal variations (differ*e*nce and differ*a*nce, in Derridian terms). While human discourse and human truth exist through difference (*écart significatif*, the difference that makes a difference), divine discourse annihilates all difference.

As has already been implied, Pascal's own discourse about Scriptural discourse itself exhibits some of the same characteristics it describes. The *Pensées* imitate the word of the Bible, as the Bible imitates the Word of God, but in neither case does charity come close to clarity. Since what is clear to God is by nature unclear to man, the only way to communicate the scandalous fact of God's existence is through techniques of obfuscation: paradox, circularity, tautology. Christ, as quoted by Pascal, speaks in paradoxes: "For whoever will save his life shall lose it" (Mark 8:35)... "Lambs did not take away the sins of the world but I am 'the lamb that taketh away the sins of the world'" (John 1:29 [L782, B818]). Pascal, in his commentary on such passages, writes in circles: "Tous ces passages ensemble peuvent être dits de la figure; donc ils ne sont pas dits de la réalité mais de la figure" [L259, B685]). This kind of reasoning would make a logician blanch; we are very far, apparently, from the methodical proofs of Pascal's own *Esprit de géométrie*. Such circular argumentation only makes sense if one is prepared to enter into a system of discourse where everything means the same thing. In other words, Pascal's circular reasoning is a figure for the unimaginable circularity of divine discourse. It is a Moebius strip turning eternally upon itself, or in Pascal's image, "Une sphere infinie dont le centre est partout, la circonférence nulle part" (L199, B72).

In his *Confessions*, Augustine conveys a similar thought through a contrasting image, drawn from James 1 (1:8): "But I hungered and thirsted not after those first works of thine [the heavens, the earth] but after thee, O Truth, with whom there is not variableness, neither shadow of turning" (III.vi.117). While Pascal's image conveys the infinite universe spinning upon itself, and Augustine's a neo-Platonic immobility, both visions are essentially mystical. Lacking any mystic credentials, I humbly descend from these dizzying heights. For me, it is enough that these mysterious phrases continue to figure the mystery of language itself.

5. La Bruyère's Perishable Words

In *Les Mots et les choses*, Michel Foucault makes the powerful assertion that the key to knowledge in any period is language. In other words, the way in which language is conceived and ordered supplies the pattern on which all knowledge is conceived and ordered. What better author through whom to explore this assertion than La Bruyère — the most language-conscious of writers in a language-conscious century, a writer who, throughout his work, comments and reflects on discourse in all its forms, from the tragedy to the cliché? Yet from the beginning, many have objected that La Bruyère's writing lacks an essential element of writing, and of thought: order. According to the *Mercure Galant*, his book is a book only by virtue of its cover.

> L'ouvrage de M de La Bruyère ne peut être appelé livre, que parce qu'il a une couverture et qu'il est relié comme les autres livres. Ce n'est qu'un amas de pièces détachées, qui ne peut faire connaître si celui qui les a faites avait assez de génie et de lumières pour bien conclure un ouvrage qui serait suivi. Rien n'est plus aisé que de faire trois ou quatre pages d'un Portrait, qui ne demande point d'ordre, et il n'y a point de génie si borné qui ne soit capable de coudre ensemble quelques médisances de son prochain et d'y ajouter ce qui lui paraît capable de faire rire. (*Mercure Galant* [juin 1693] 271-72. Quoted in Servois II.193)

As this quotation shows, almost from their publication, La Bruyère's *Caractères* drew criticism for their apparent lack of structure. Neither a unified book nor a collection of essays, the *Caractères* are an amalgam of disparate *remarques* (as La Bruyère first called them) whose interrelation is difficult to assess. The editors of the *Mercure Galant*, from which the above criticism is taken, spare La Bruyère no sarcasm. Doubtless, his devastating judgment on their own publication still rankled. "Le M* G* est immédiatement audessus de rien" (*Des Ouvrages de l'esprit* 46). Contemporary polemics aside, even less biased and more reflective critics like Boileau found the *Caractères* structurally weak. Boileau claimed that La Bruyère's style "était prophétique, qu'il fallait souvent le deviner; qu'un ouvrage comme le sien ne demandait que de l'esprit, puis qu'il délivrait de la servitude des transitions" (*Bolaeana* 410). As Boileau perceptively points out, while the creation of continuity in a work may be a *pierre d'achoppement* for the writer, elliptical style is especially a problem for the reader.

In fact, the history of La Bruyère criticism can be seen as an effort to restructure and redefine his work into a more comfortably assimilable, readable form. Many of these efforts have been negative, like the *Mercure Galant's* reduction of the *Caractères* to "quelques médisances sur son prochain," or unproductive, like the searches for *clés* to the alleged models for La Bruyère's portraits. As the abbé d'Olivet noted in 1729, this strategy for reading soon outlived its usefulness: "tant qu'on a cru voir dans ce livre les portraits de gens vivants, on l'a dévoré, pour se nourrir du triste plaisir que donne la satire personnelle; mais à mesure que ces gens-là ont disparu, il a cessé de plaire si fort par la matière, et peut-être aussi que la forme n'a pas suffi toute seule pour le sauver, quoiqu'il soit plein de tours admirables et d'expressions heureuses que n'étoient pas dans notre langue auparavant" (*Histoire de l'Académie française* II.319). But the Abbé's funeral oration was premature; the *Caractères* continue to be read, and to engage and irritate their readers.

Suard, who edited La Bruyère in the early nineteenth century, agrees that "on est moins frappé des pensées que du style" (Notice 7). However, he attempts to counter Boileau's criticism: "Despréaux observait, à ce qu'on dit, que La Bruyère, en évitant les transitions, s'étoit épargné ce qu'il y a de plus difficile dans un ouvrage. Cette observation ne me paroît pas digne d'un si grand maître. Il saurait trop bien qu'il y a dans l'art d'écrire des secrets plus importants que celui de trouver ces formules qui servent à lier les idées, et à réunir les parties du discours." He adds, interestingly, "Ce n'est point sans doute pour éviter les transitions que La Bruyère a écrit son livre par fragments et par pensées détachées. Ce plan convenoit mieux à son objet" (10-11). But he does not elaborate this notion. Sainte-Beuve, however, did: "Chez lui, le manque absolu de transition est souvent un calcul de l'art" (*Les Grands Ecrivains français* III.187-88). He also remarks: "La composition, pour être dissimulée, n'en est point absente" ("Les *Caractères* de La Bruyère," *Nouveaux Lundis* I.129).

In our times the structure of the work continues to provoke mixed feelings. While admiring the *Caractères*' portrayal of society, Louis van Delft criticizes their overall composition.

> D'un côté, La Bruyère se livre donc sur le réel à une opération purement arbitraire et intellectuelle. Il aboutit à une désintégration de la réalité vivante, qu'il fragmente à l'infini. ... Puis, dans cet ensemble disparate, il introduit seize points fixes, choisis sans originalité, et très scolastiquement imposés à cette réalité désagrégée, au lieu de se dégager d'elle. (*La Bruyère moraliste* 63)

For van Delft, La Bruyère is alternately rigid and fanciful, subjective and objective, a strange combination of natural scientist and impressionist painter:

> Il n'adopte, pour peindre les hommes, aucun angle privilégié, à la manière d'un Bossuet écrivant l'Histoire. Il brosse de la société un tableau purement impressioniste, ne suit que sa verve ou son caprice, et aboutit à une fragmentation, à une divergence illimitées. (54)

If La Bruyère has disconcerted generations of readers, it is easy to see why. He substitutes juxtaposition for logical development: neither continuous nor totally discontinuous, his writing proceeds by fits and starts. The narrative perspective shifts back and forth between general observation and barely sketched illustration; fantastic, ephemeral figures appear and disappear with dizzying rapidity, but never really come to life. Thus, La Bruyère's writing flouts traditional notions of verisimilitude. The reader seeks for a solid imitation of reality to which he can cling and finds only fragments. Indeed, fragmentation is the defining stylistic feature of the *Caractères*. The text is an epic accumulation of fragments: from year to year, from edition to edition, it grew in snail-like accretions, inexhaustible as La Bruyère's subject itself. For the description of human behavior — *les moeurs de ce siècle* — is an infinite task. Like Achilles in Zeno's paradox, the moralist can never reach his goal; he can only achieve successive approximations which are "plus complet, plus fini, plus régulier."[1] More and more and more, fragments upon fragments.

[1] La Bruyère, *Les Caractères*, ed. R. Garapon (Paris: Garnier, 1962), Préface 65. Further references will appear in the text.

This apparent *parti-pris* of fragmentation has posed perhaps the greatest obstacle to La Bruyère's acceptance as a serious author. While critics have often found his *style coupé* intriguing, they have also found it an impediment to comprehension. Instead of presenting his ideas in a coherent, linear fashion, La Bruyère perversely entangles the reader in a web of inconsistencies and contradictions. Even for a sensitive modern reader like Odette de Mourgues, La Bruyère remains a puzzle and a paradox: "A touch of immediacy has been added which combines paradoxically with an impression of total unreality... La Bruyère is famous for his portraits. Are they, paradoxically, portraits of invisible men?" (Two French Moralists 153-62). Earlier generations of critics, less patient with La Bruyère's vagaries, demoted him to the rank of "stylist," meaning that he had no ideas at all, or at least none of his own. In Faguet's devastating formula, "il usa d'un style tout nouveau pour ne rien dire de très nouveau."[2] From this abstract separation between style and content, it was easy to proceed to the actual physical dislocation of the text itself. *Le style coupé invite au découpage*: La Bruyère's already disjointed work was further dismembered into anthology pieces, to supply students with food for style, if not for thought. Of all classical authors, La Bruyère seemed most destined to serve out his days in *morceaux choisis*. He even predicted the annihilation of his own text: "Il n'y a pas d'ouvrage si accompli qu'il ne fondît tout entier au milieu de la critique" (*Des Ouvrages de l'esprit* 26).

However, some now see things differently. La Bruyère's choppy style, which bemused earlier readers, looks comfortably "modern" to Roland Barthes.[3] For him, La Bruyère's writing invites us to see it *as* writing; his *caractères* are not characters in a solid nineteenth-century sense, but literary apparitions, phantoms of language. Viewed from this perspective, fragmentation does not weaken the *Caractères*. Instead, it constitutes their very textuality. While earlier critics talked in essentially negative terms of *style coupé* and *morcellement*, Barthes and Doubrovsky[4] speak of juxtaposition and parataxis. In other words,

[2] *Dix-septième siècle* (Paris: Société Française d'Imprimerie, n.d.) 492. For the reception of the *Caractères*, see Jules Brody, "La Bruyère: le style d'un moraliste," *CAIEF* 30 (May 1978) 139-41, and Jacqueline Hellegouarc'h, *La Phrase dans 'Les Caractères' de La Bruyère* (Paris: Champion, 1975) 1-4.

[3] "Du mythe à l'écriture," Preface to *Les Caractères* 17. Interestingly, La Bruyère's style was criticized for its "modernism" in the late seventeenth century.

[4] "Lecture de La Bruyère," *Poétique* 2 (1970) 198.

they see fragmentation as a positive feature of style, a presence rather than an absence, a generic principle which links together a variety of forms often relegated to *morceaux choisis*. Like *caractères*, *maximes*, *réflexions*, *pensées*, and *portraits* resist a synthetic approach. All these forms call for a new interpretive method, an esthetics of fragmentation[5] that would take discontinuity as a stylistic given with its own thematic consequences.

Such an esthetics might begin by addressing the following questions: How do we define the textual unit in a fragmented work? Do traditional labels like *portrait* or *maxime* convey useful stylistic distinctions? What is the relation between the fragment and its textual environment? Do fragments contrast with one another, overlap like waves on a beach, or meet in pointillistic juxtaposition? Or does the concept of fragmentation really suit La Bruyère's writing? Finally — and we can ask this question as often as we like because it will never be definitely answered: What line can be drawn from style to thought? Can we say that a shattered form implies a shattered vision and, if so, can we justifiably go further, as Doubrovsky does, and see in La Bruyère's style "le tragique moderne de l'écriture?" (201).

I will approach these theoretical questions on several levels, beginning by examining three consecutive passages from the *Caractères* (*De la cour* 81-83). I have deliberately chosen an excerpt which is not a *morceau d'anthologie* or even a portrait, and is therefore more representative of La Bruyère's writing as a whole. Moreover, this is an essential passage for studying the phenomenon of fragmentation because it deals with the dislocation and disappearance of language itself. In an inexorable progression, social language (*les phrases toutes faites* [81]), esthetic language (*cinq ou six termes de l'art* [82]) are first reduced to caricatures and then to silence (*ils plaisent à force de se taire* [83]). My analysis will bear mainly on 81, with some incursions into succeeding *caractères*; although one cannot look for linear continuity in La Bruyère, one can identify clusters of related elements, and this is such a cluster. After examining the overall structure of 81, I will analyze its syntax and vocabulary. In light of this analysis, and with some La Bruyèrian *va-et-vient* between description and observation, I will consider the relation of language to ideology in the text and make an assessment of its modernity.

[5] Dominique Secretan talks about an esthetics of fragmentation in his introduction to La Rochefoucauld, *Réflexions ou sentences et maximes morales* (Geneva: Droz, 1967)

> Il y a un certain nombre de phrases toutes faites, que l'on prend comme dans un magasin, et dont l'on se sert pour se féliciter les uns des autres sur les événements; bien qu'elles se disent souvent sans affection et qu'elles soient reçues sans reconnaissance il n'est pas permis avec cela de les omettre, parce que du moins elles sont l'image de ce qu'il y a au monde de meilleur, qui est l'amitié, et que les hommes, ne pouvant guère compter les uns sur les autres pour la réalité, semblent être convenus entre eux de se contenter des apparences. (*De la cour* 81)

The first thing to remark about this passage is its unremarkableness. The unmistakable stamp of the author is lacking; on reading it, one does not exclaim: "c'est du La Bruyère." In style, it is apparently a piece of "straight" classical prose, brief, concise and abstract. Unlike better-known passages, it contains no extravagant images, but many generalizations and impersonal expressions (*il y a*, *il n'est pas permis*, *l'on prend*, *l'on se sert*). To the extent that these terms have usefulness, it is a *maxime*, not a *portrait*. Instead of linguistic expansiveness, there is a sense of reduction, almost of penury: *un certain nombre de phrases toutes faites* (81) or *cinq ou six termes de l'art, et rien de plus* (82) serve all communicative needs. It is as if there are hardly enough words to go around; they must be hoarded (*enmagasiné*) and recycled indefinitely.

On a structural level, similar effects of limitation and closure prevail. Rather than as a *maxime* or *reflection*, it is fruitful to think of *De la cour* 81 as a classical period. Etymologically, "period" denotes circularity and containment (*peri-od*, a way around). It is a circumscribed unit, a prisonyard of discourse. It is also a form which draws its own conclusions, down to the *pointe finale*, the sting in its tail. Doubrovsky (198-99) has noted the verse-like periodicity of La Bruyère's final cadences. This effect is muted in 81, but very strong in 83, which ends with a perfect alexandrine: "si vous les enfoncez, vous rencontrez le tuff."

At the same time, the outward coherence of the period is dependent on an inner discontinuity. According to Littré, the period is both *assemblage* and *ensemble*, "un assemblage de propositions liées entre elles par des conjonctions, et qui toutes ensemble font un sens fini, dit aussi complet." The whole is clearly greater than the sum of its separate

xix, but appears to restrict its meaning to formal aspects of the work. Philip Lewis discusses the problem of fragmentation in *La Rochefoucauld: The Art of Abstraction* (Ithaca: Cornell University Press, 1977) 42-54.

parts, but the process by which *assemblage* becomes *ensemble* remains mysterious. Condillac, in *L'Art d'écrire*, emphasizes the same ambivalence: "Tous les membres [de la période] doivent être *distincts et liés les uns aux autres*; quand ces conditions ne sont pas remplies, ce n'est plus qu'un assemblage confus de plusieurs phrases."[6] The integration of the period is also separation; in syntax as in art, *solitaire* is *solidaire.*[7]

These observations on periodic style also apply to La Bruyère's text on a global level. In the *Caractères*, the relation between continuity and discontinuity is not antithetic, but dialectic. Passages of differing length and structure play off against one another. In general, short periodic fragments like *De la cour* 81 form a background against which the longer, more flamboyant fragments stand out. These shorter passages remain a constant in La Bruyère's production: although the proportion of short fragments in editions 1-4 seems higher than in later editions, new short passages continue to appear. A thorough study of "contextuality" in the *Caractères* would take into account their special rhythm of expansion and contraction, opening and closing.

De la cour 81 is also periodic in the detail of its syntax. While in other passages — *De la cour* 32, for example — La Bruyère's "diluvial sentences" are built upon a series of enumerations,[8] the structural principle in 81 is subordination. The passage consists of a single sentence which, to the modern reader, appears too long, or of two sentences, breaking before *bien que*. Punctuation practice varies from edition to edition, from period to colon to semicolon, but in any case the two basic elements of the passage are held together by strong syntactic linkage. A grammatical diagram of the passage would reveal a complex structure of parallels and subordinates (see fig. 6). The first phrase (*il y a* ...) begins with an independent clause, followed by two subordinates which (chrono)logically divide the subject. First, we are told where ready-made phrases come from (*comme dans un magasin*); then, what they are used for (*se féliciter* ...). The second phrase has a triadic structure, with an independent clause (*il* ... *omettre*) placed between

[6] Quoted in Littré under *période*. I was unable to find an original source for this quotation.

[7] In Camus' short story "Jonas," included in *L'Exil et le royaume* (Paris: Gallimard, 1967) 176, an artist writes on his canvas a single word which can be read as either *solitaire* or *solidaire*.

[8] On La Bruyère's diluviality, see Jules Brody, "Sur le style de La Bruyère," *Esprit Créateur* 2.2 (Summer 1971) 154, 165.

```
        6
Il y a . . . . . . faites,
                              5
                |/que . . . . . magasin,
                |/et dont . . . . . . . . . .
                              10       /sur les événements:

                    3          2
           2        il . . .         . . omettre,                      12
bien qu'elles se disent . . .  [avec cela]   |/parce que . . . . . . . . . . . . . . . . . . . . . . . . . . . meilleur,
     |/et qu'elles . . . .                   |                                                      [qui est l'amitié]
           4                                 |/et que les hommes,
                                                    [ne . . . . . . . . . . . . . . . . . . . . . . . . réalité,]*
                                                                    10
                                       3
                              *semblent . . . eux
                                                    3
                                              /de . . . apparences.


        independent clause                         [elements in apposition]
                  |/parallel
                  |/   subordinate clauses

        Numbers indicate words in ellipsis.
```

Figure 6

two sets of dependent clauses, the former in the subjunctive, the latter in the indicative mode. The indicative clauses (*parce que* ... *et que* ...) each contain elements in apposition (*qui est l'amitié, ne* ... *réalité*). The two main parts of the passage are linked together by this use of apposition: *qui est l'amitié* refers back ironically to *sans affection*, and *ne pouvant guère compter les uns sur les autres* comments on *dont l'on se sert pour se féliciter les uns des autres*, in a critical echo.

This syntactic analysis reveals a close-knit structure with many elements of symmetry. If the symmetry is not immediately apparent, perhaps it is because La Bruyère assiduously avoids parallel elements of the same length. For example, of the two clauses in apposition, one has four words, the other twelve. His avoidance of obvious patterning is conscious: "Le commun des hommes aime les phrases et les périodes," and La Bruyère is not writing for the common man. The result is a style which disguises its own structural coherence.

The structure of the passage also highlights its theme: the *déclassement* of court language. In the first phrase, syntactic breaks occur after *phrases toutes faites* and *dans un magasin*, two expressions which place language in a commercial context. *Magasin*, according to Littré, is "un lieu où l'on garde des marchandises," coming from the Arabic *khazan*, to gather or accumulate. *Le commerce de la vie* (*comme on disait au dix-septième siècle*) goes on at Versailles as it does in a *tapissier*'s shop; courtiers, like petit-bourgeois shopkeepers, hoard verbal goods and use them to meet their social obligations. But unlike a self-respecting *tapissier*, a courtier often pays his debts with shoddy merchandise (*phrases toutes faites*).

This is wonderful social satire; but more than that, La Bruyère's *magasin de phrases* contains, *en raccourci*, an implicit theory of language. To translate his elegant metaphor into inelegant "social sciencese," speech is a para-economic exchange system which follows the contractual norms of commerce. In everyday life, people trade words, gestures, and smiles for many cogent reasons having little to do with primary communication: to preserve or advance their position, to impress others, to strengthen their self-image, or simply to earn a living. These verbal exchanges are represented in the text by reciprocal and reflexive constructions: *se féliciter les uns des autres*, *compter les uns sur les autres*. Such expressions are so common not only in this passage but throughout the *Caractères*, that one could almost say with La Bruyère, "tout est réciproque" (*De la société* 45).

La Bruyère's reciprocal system interestingly prefigures an insight of structural anthropology. For example, Claude Lévi-Strauss has commented on the custom of exchanging wine in little *provençal* restaurants[9]: "voulez-vous goûter de mon vin?" says one customer to another, holding up a bottle of *vin ordinaire* not very different from, or perhaps identical to the other's. And the second diner reciprocates. From observing this custom, Lévi-Strauss concludes that more is involved in the act of exchange than the thing exchanged — in this case, nearly identical wine. La Bruyère would have concurred: just as *convives* in French restaurants are exchanging something other than wine, people engaged in polite conversation are exchanging something other than words.

While La Bruyère is enough of an anthropologist to have anticipated Lévi-Strauss' insight, he remains enough of a moralist to regret the absence of authentic communication. Once words become part of an economic exchange system, they are subject to inflation; and, for La Bruyère, verbal coinage has become so debased as to have lost almost all content. In describing language, La Bruyère places the emphasis not on the message conveyed but on its production — on the *speech act*, as linguistics now call it. Thus, the stranger who eavesdrops on a Paris *côterie* "voit un peuple qui cause, bourdonne, parle à l'oreille, éclate de rire, et qui retombe ensuite dans un morne silence" (*De la ville* 13). Speech, reduced to pure act, is the functional equivalent of silence: *on se parle sans se rien dire*. In this perspective, *les phrases toutes faites* — the workaday language of polite society — hardly aspires to imitate real communication: like the *faux brillants* of costume jewelry, speech is meant to dazzle, not to fool.

Erica Harth has related the devaluation of classical language to the *déclassement* of the nobility in the early modern period ("Classical Disproportion" 189-210). When impoverished nobles sell their estates or their daughters to affluent bourgeois, and bourgeois buy offices which confer quasi-noble rank, the whole social order is thrown into crisis. And since people live by the symbols they create, this social crisis also entails a crisis of language. What can it mean to be "noble," or to speak of "noble sentiments," if nobility, once a moral quality, has become a salable item? And how can an exchange of nobility for money maintain an authentic reciprocity? When Molière's Dom Juan rewards his creditors with compliments, *payer de mots* becomes a way to get something for nothing. "*Les Caractères* décrivent un monde ... privé de métaphysique, monde où le métaphysique a cédé la place

[9] Dennis Tedlock, lecture on Lévi-Strauss, University Professor's Seminar on Translation, Boston University, 20 October 1978.

au physique, monde délaissé par l'esprit et abandonné désormais à la matière sous toutes ses multiples manifestations, monde livré à l'or, à ce et à ceux que l'or achète" (Brody 167). In a world where everything is for sale, including oneself, *payer de mots*, or even *de mines* (*De la cour* 83), are logical strategies for survival.

And yet, while exposing the fraudulence of social discourse, La Bruyère does not totally empty it of content. *La politesse* remains *l'image de l'amitié*, and poor as the likeness is, we must make do with it, in honor of the absent reality. Nor, strictly speaking, is the reality totally absent: for La Bruyère — and in this respect he remains profoundly classical — the moral order maintains a real, if marginal, existence. In *De la cour* 81, the operative adverbs are *souvent ... guère*, not *toujours ... jamais*: La Bruyère's friendship, like Pascal's God, is almost, but not quite, invisible (*il se cache ordinairement et se découvre rarement*).[10] On a linguistic level, a similar dynamic applies: the link between language and its moral referent is nearly, but not entirely, effaced. This alienation of word from referent is reflected in the syntax of the passage: all allusions to moral/psychological *réalités* appear either in the negative, as in the first phrase (*sans affection*), or in apposition, as in the second (*qui est l'amitié*). In La Bruyère's *magasin*, authentic feelings are shelved, tantalizingly, just out of reach.

We have already referred to the "classical ideology of representation"[11] — words representing things — but La Bruyère's linguistic principle is closer to *suppléance* (substitution). Words, or extra-linguistic signs (*ils payent de mines, de voix, d'un geste, et d'un sourire*) take the place of something else that is hardly ever there: friendship, esthetic knowledge, intelligence, virtue. Or, if one wishes, La Bruyère retains the notion of representation while dislocating it. His representation is re-presentation at one remove: words represent not things communicated, but communication itself.

In this passage, La Bruyère moves from the "deconstruction" of social language to its partial recuperation. Like Pierre Nicole's *civilité chrétienne*, *l'échange de phrases toutes faites* is a profane social ritual performed in the name of a higher value. Once primary communication

[10] Pascal, letter to Mlle de Roannez, October 1656, in *Oeuvres complètes* (Paris: Seuil, 1963) 267.

[11] Cf., for example, Jean Lafond: "L'art classique est art de la représentation: la première qualité d'une oeuvre est d'atteindre à la 'vérité' de l'objet représenté, que cet objet soit pensée ou chose" (*L'Avant-propos* to Jules Brody, *Du style à la pensée: trois études sur les Caractères de La Bruyère* [Lexington, Kentucky: French Forum, 1980]).

has been discredited, the only consolation we can still offer one another is the exchange of polite phrases — the cold comfort of a warm breath. La Bruyère gives this exchange the force of a moral imperative in the maxim-like phrase, "Il n'est pas permis avec cela de les omettre." But the basic maxim structure — "il n'est pas permis … de les omettre" — is literally broken by the interjection *avec cela*, which brings back to mind the insufficiencies of language so tellingly revealed in the first part of the fragment. La Bruyère's syntax bears the weight of his disabused morality; he knows too much to write an unbroken *sentence*.

With periodic logic, we have returned to our point of departure: the esthetics of fragmentation in La Bruyère. *De la cour* 81 figures in microcosm the dilemma La Bruyère faces as a moralist and as a writer. If social language is a *magasin*, the *Caractères* themselves can be likened to a *grand magasin*, an *étalage* of facts, portraits and visions which do not form a coherent whole. The moralist cannot create an integral view of society when there is no solid foundation on which to build, when moral discourse itself is counterfeit. La Bruyère's response to this dilemma is, in the end, a writer's response. All he can do is to construct a well-made individual text, which will give the lie to the shoddy language surrounding him. The difference between La Bruyère's own *magasin* and the one he describes is analogous to the difference between hand-crafted and industrialized manufacture, *phrases faites à la main* and *phrases toutes faites*. La Bruyère's painstaking craftsmanship represents a return, at least on a metaphoric level, to a pre-capitalist ethic of production: *c'est un métier de faire un livre comme de faire une pendule*. But La Bruyère's concern for language, whatever its economic implications, demonstrates a strong moral commitment: he is a moralist by being a stylist. There is no need to reconcile these two terms, if indeed their contradiction exists outside the mind of critics. Texts, like people, live their own contradictions, live with them and through them; and La Bruyère's characters will continue to live their lives beyond the half-lives of our interpretations.

Having seen how La Bruyère puts a paragraph together — which he does admirably — let us see how he assembles a chapter. I have chosen "De la Société et de la conversation" because it deals explicitly with social language. The chapter possesses a fairly coherent theme: for society to function adequately, it is necessary to know how — and how not — to speak. Unfortunately, for La Bruyère, the failures of social intercourse outnumber the successes. The chapter abounds in descriptions of those ubiquitous *fâcheux* and trouble-makers who make social life less than ideal. It begins and ends with an experience one does not seek, but often finds, in society: boredom. The first *remarque* — "Un caractère bien fade est celui de n'en avoir aucun" — is echoed by the last: "Le sage quelquefois évite le monde, de peur d'être ennuyé." This last aphorism confirms the playfully moralistic tone of the whole: it is something of a cliché that the wise man avoids society, but not for the reason given.

Thus, in a world-weary tone almost parodic of the *moraliste*, the chapter begins with what is unpleasant and in poor taste in society (2-6). These unpleasantnesses are mostly verbal, and lend themselves to longer interpolations (7-9). In Remarks 10 and 11, this initial pattern breaks down; 10 discusses the way to conduct a conversation and 11 turns the attention to language itself: "combien de ces mots aventuriers qui paraissent subitement, durent un temps, et que bientôt on ne revoit plus. ..." Remark 11 also makes the transition back to the *fâcheux*, such as the loud-speaking Théodecte (12) and the interfering Troïle (13), a Tartuffe-like character who dominates another's household. Remarks 14 and 15 deal with people who talk indiscreetly or too much, while 16-21 reverse the coin to discuss the art of conversation itself. Remark 22 returns by negative example to a portrait of poor speaking: "Cléan parle peu obligeamment ou peu juste, c'est l'un ou l'autre." Remark 23 is an abstract reflection on good speaking, illustrated by a portrait in 24. In Remarks 25-28, La Bruyère shows how social contact fails when speech fails. Here, as elsewhere, the two are inseparably linked: "Parler et offenser, pour de certaines gens, est précisément la même chose" (27). Remarks 29-30 also deal with the failure of social contact. Remark 31 introduces the topic of manners or politeness, and its indispensability in a social setting; this topic is continued through 34. Remarks 35 and 36 are less classifiable; then 37 introduces again the topic of handling *fâcheux*. Remark 38 begins a long section on quarrels and ways in which people fail to get along, which leads into remarks on the pettiness and gossipy spirit of the provinces (49-51). Remarks 52-53, again, escape easy classification, as does 58. Remarks 54-57, in between, deal with laughter; 59-60 with disdain. Remarks 61-62 treat good society and how to get along in it. Remarks 63-64 deal with giving advice; 65 with a satire of the Précieuses and their search for an exaggerated finesse of expression. Remark 66, in portrait form, satirizes an aging *bel esprit*. Remarks 68-70 continue the critique of overly refined conversation begun in 65, while 71-74 give other examples of antisocial speech, crudeness and pedantry. Remark 75 stands out from its context as a portrait of the *esprit de contradiction*; 76-78 discuss tone and manner of speaking, while 79-81 deal with secrecy. Finally, La Bruyère paints a portrait of his last *fâcheux*, an old suitor who tells more than one wants to know about his finances, family connections and so forth.

This rapid analysis of "De la Société" shows it is far from the inchoate mass some critics seem to discern in the *Caractères*. The chapter possesses a basic thematic structure, with an oscillation between positive and negative examples of social and verbal behavior. However, certain passages such as 35-36, 52-53, or 75, do not easily fit into this structure. Most striking, there is little smooth flow from one remark to another, and sometimes no flow at all. The work constantly sets up, then violates, its own expectations. Instead of developing a subject and linking it to the next, La Bruyère interrupts or drops it. Rather than no order, it supplies just enough order to make us wish for more.

Thus, the discomfort the reader feels with *Les Caractères* is apparently inscribed in its structure. The text will not accept a conventional order or submit to a linear type of reading. A similar sense of incompleteness, of indefiniteness also permeates the text stylistically. In remarks that do not contain portraits, La Bruyère often uses the indefinite article: "Des gens vous promettent le secret" (81). This usage is also combined with *il y a*: "Il y a des gens d'une certaine étoffe" (238); "Il y a des gens qui parlent un moment avant que d'avoir pensé" (15); "Il y a beaucoup d'esprits obscènes" (4). Other delimiting, yet general, expressions reinforce the impression that society is an ocean where the writer casts out nets without being exactly sure what he will catch each time: "certains esprits"; "cet inconnu." As La Bruyère himself points out in a remark quoted earlier (11), language itself appears and disappears without one really knowing where it has gone.

These structural and stylistic discontinuities are in keeping with La Bruyère's vision of social conversation: "l'on suit ses idées, et on les explique sans le moindre égard pour les raisonnements d'autrui; l'on est bien éloigné de trouver ensemble la vérité, l'on n'est pas encore convenu de celle qu'on cherche. Qui pourrait écouter ces sortes de conversations *et les écrire*, ferait voir quelque fois de bonnes choses qui n'ont nulle suite" (67, emphasis mine). This passage shows La Bruyère fully cognizant of the difficulties of his own project. It is not that he is incapable of writing *avec suite*. But while the "pure" moralist expresses the truth, or a truth, in logical order, the writer who wishes to portray the real operation of society rather than how it should operate, must develop new techniques which violate the continuity we expect from reading. Hence, the self-contained and discontinuous form of the *caractère* both reveals the problematic nature of social description and proposes an innovative, if not wholly satisfying, solution: as Diderot will do with the biological sciences a century later, in *Le Rêve d'Alembert*, La Bruyère suggests that new knowledge of ourselves and the world – a presocial science, if you will – cannot be expressed in traditional discursive forms.

From these obervations, is it possible to take a further step and posit *Les Caractères* as a "sociological" text: one belonging, in La Bruyère's words, to *cette science qui décrit les moeurs*? Of course, it is also an *oeuvre de morale*, enjoying a complex status where description and prescription, portrayal and instruction are blended in proportions difficult to determine. But no one would deny that the *Caractères* are full of observations of contemporary manners and reflections on society, and some of these may constitute a kind of presocial science. For example, this passage from the *Discours sur Théophraste* almost prefigures Montesquieu's *Lettres persanes*:

> Que si quelques-uns se refroidissaient pour cet ouvrage moral par les choses qu'ils y voient, qui sont du temps auquel il a été écrit, et qui ne sont point selon leurs moeurs, que peuvent-ils faire de plus utile et de plus agréable pour eux que de se défaire de cette prévention pour leurs coutumes et leurs manières, qui, sans autre discussion, non seulement les leur fait trouver les meilleures de toutes, mais leur fait presque décider que tout ce qui n'est pas conforme est méprisable, et qui les prive, dans la lecture des livres des anciens, du plaisir et de l'instruction qu'ils en doivent attendre? (10)

Without Montesquieu's concrete historical sense, La Bruyère does suggest a kind of relativism which would affect one's reading.

If the *Caractères* do contain a form of social knowledge, how is it organized? Among possible models of order, we can immediately eliminate the chronological: for La Bruyère, temporal order is not a possible way to *faire l'histoire du monde présent*, as he calls it. The other models of order I will consider fall into two categories: analytic and classificatory. I use the term "analytic" in a specific sense of the procedure Descartes outlines in his *Discours de la méthode*: linear ordering on a mathematical model, where one breaks the material up into its smallest elements and puts them into ascending order. In Descartes' words, "Conduire ses pensées par ordre, en commençant par les objets les plus simples et les plus aisés à connaître, pour monter peu à peu et comme par degrés jusqu'à la connaissance des plus composés, en supposant même de l'ordre entre ceux qui ne se précèdent point naturellement les uns les autres" (IV). Pierre Laubriet claims that this same procedure was followed by La Bruyère: "en même temps qu'il augmenta son ouvrage, il y mit de l'ordre, en classique qu'il était" (Laubriet 512). Louis van Delft also comments explicitly on the Cartesianism of La Bruyère. Other readers, however, emphatically deny any relation between Cartesian analysis and La Bruyère in particular or classical social description in general. Thus, according to Ernst Cassirer in *Philosophy of the Enlightenment*, historical, factual knowledge is not susceptible to Cartesian ordering. Cartesianism "remained aloof from the sphere of history. According to this philosophy, nothing merely factual can claim any real certainty, and no kind of factual knowledge can be compared in value to the clear and distinct knowledge of logic, to pure mathematics, and to the exact natural sciences" (201).

Without taking a position on this issue at the moment, I will pass on to the second model: taxonomic order, or classification. In *Science and the Modern World*, Alfred North Whitehead calls classification a "halfway house between the immediate concreteness of the individual theory and the complete abstraction of mathematical notions" (30). Like Cassirer, he implies that classification is methodologically inferior to mathematical measurement. Classification nonetheless remains the major way of organizing factual material in the social sciences. I will discuss two forms of classification, the first of which is deductive or Aristotelian. I will examine Aristotelian classification in some detail since La Bruyère actually cites Aristotle as the source of Theophrastus' *Characters*.

Although Aristotle's scientific classification is somewhat different from his moral and esthetic categories, both share a basic unifying principle. Scientific knowledge, or *episteme* in the Aristotelian sense, is a demonstrative connection between substances (subjects) and their attributes (predicates). These form a syllogistic, tripartite structure. Human knowledge, whether theoretical or practical, can be completely subsumed under this deductive arrangement. The difference is one of aim (in ethics, to help people behave better) rather than method. The Nichomachean *Ethics* II contains a table of virtues which groups moral characteristics into all-embracing categories. Each virtue is seen as the mean between two extremes: thus, modesty is the mean between shyness (excess) and shamelessness (deficiency). In III-IV, each virtue is embodied in a generalized social type: the wise man, the boastful man, the buffoon, and so forth. Aristotle does say that the extravagant man spends too much money on trivial causes such as lavishly equipping the comic chorus in the theater (IV.2), but this kind of concrete detail is rare; it is the kind of detail Theophrastus will supply.

The second type of classification of relevance to La Bruyère is the inductive or encyclopedic. Encyclopedias and dictionaries are a relatively new phenomenon. Dating from the Renaissance, they are based on a new model of order which is not logical but spatial; relations between terms involve juxtaposition and contiguity rather than deduction. In the *Encyclopédie*, Diderot and d'Alembert use the phrase *mappemonde des connaissances* to describe their enterprise. The implication is that the relation between categories is less important than the all-inclusiveness of the structural scheme: like the paint in the old Sherwin Williams ad, it should cover the earth. Cassirer, in the work already cited, says of Pierre Bayle: "It is no accident that he chose for his critical work the form of a *Historical and Critical Dictionary*. For the dictionary allows the spirit of mere coordination to prevail by contrast with the spirit of subordination that dominates the rational systems" (202). Rational systems would include, of course, both Cartesian analysis and Aristotelian deduction. He continues, "In Bayle there is no hierarchy of concepts, no deductive derivation of one concept from another, but rather a simple aggregation of materials, each of which is as significant as any other and shares with it an equal claim to complete and exhaustive treatment... Frequently the most insignificant subjects, or even completely nonsensical ones, are treated in the *Dictionary* elaborately and conscientiously, while most important matters are neglected" (202). Cassirer's comments on Bayle, with their blend of fascination and annoyance, could have been written about La Bruyère.

What does La Bruyère himself have to say about this matter? Both the Preface and the *Discours sur Théophraste* contain explicit remarks on the structure of his work. La Bruyère begins the *Discours* by remarking, aptly, that it is vain to try to please all one's readers. Even if one limits the case to *ouvrages de morale* (*cette science qui décrit les moeurs*) people have widely different expectations of what such works should contain:

> Enfin quelle apparence de pouvoir remplir tous les goûts si différents des hommes par un seul ouvrage de morale? Les uns cherchent des définitions, des divisions, des tables, et de la méthode: ils veulent qu'on leur explique ce que c'est que la vertu en général, et cette vertu en par-

> ticulier; quelle différence se trouve entre la valeur, la force, et la magnanimité; les vices extrêmes par le défaut ou par l'excès entre lesquels chaque vertu se trouve placée, et duquel de ces deux extrêmes elle emprunte davantage; toute autre doctrine ne leur plaît pas. (4)

Although the note in the Garapon edition refers us to the seventeenth-century works of Coëffeteau and le Père Senault, one can recognize in this description the moral categories of Aristotle's *Ethics*. While expressing a great respect for Aristotle throughout the *Discours*, La Bruyère implicitly rejects his ethical method; readers who expect this kind of approach are portrayed as narrow-minded and rigid (*toute autre doctrine ne leur plaît pas*). Similarly, he makes fun of the Cartesian mechanical explanation of the passions: "et que l'on explique celles-ci par le mouvement du sang, par celui des fibres et des artères, quittent un auteur de tout le reste" (4-5).

The readers La Bruyère selects are *un troisième ordre* (5). In an important passage, he devalues the theoretical: "supposant les principes physiques et moraux rebattus par les anciens et les modernes" and emphasizes the empirical and the pragmatic: "Se jettent d'abord dans leur application aux moeurs du temps, corrigent les hommes les uns par les autres, par ces images de choses qui leur sont si familières..." For La Bruyère, systematic theory stands in the way of the direct contact with social reality which he seeks and which gives his writing its special vitality: as he puts it, "se jettent d'abord" — plunging right into things.

La Bruyère continues, rather deceptively, "Tel est le traité des Caractères des moeurs que nous a laissé Théophraste." This is not really the case: the ethical concern he speaks of is nearly absent from Théophraste's work, and its structure is clearer, based on a definition of each social type with illustrations. What would seem to appeal to La Bruyère, however, is the detail — "ces images de choses qui leur sont si familières." For example, speaking of stinginess, Theophrastus says, in La Bruyère's translation: "Il n'est permis à personne de cueillir une figue dans leur jardin, de passer au travers de leur champ, de ramasser une petite branche de palmier, ou quelques olives qui seront tombées de l'arbre. Ils vont tous les jours se promener sur leurs terres, en remarquent les bornes, voient si l'on n'y a rien changé et si elles sont toujours les mêmes" (34).

La Bruyère also states of Theophrastus' work: "Il l'a puisé dans les *Ethiques* et dans les *grandes Morales* d'Aristote, dont il fut le disciple." In fact, this is not exactly the case: the definitions and categories are mostly not from Aristotle, and many of them are not even by Theophrastus himself, although La Bruyère did not know it. Theophrastus' product is very different from its supposed sources. Even the word "Character" (Charakter) is not used by Aristotle. In the *Ethics*, the word Aristotle uses is *hexis*: a settled disposition or habit of mind; in the *Rhetoric*, *ethos*, in the similar sense of what is habitual or characteristic of an individual. Both these words are now translated by "character" because it has taken on a psychological meaning in modern languages.[12]

It is arguable that in describing the translation of Theophrastus, La Bruyère is actually expounding his own vision of what an *ouvrage de moeurs* should be. And, indeed, after discussing Theoprastus' life and work, La Bruyère begins to speak of his own original *remarques*. With a similar contradiction to that already observed in his treatment of Aristotle, despite his respectful treatment of the model, La Bruyère says he will not do as Theophrastus does in his *Characters*, but instead refers to an obscure and disputed work:

> L'on a cru pouvoir se dispenser de suivre le projet de ce philosophe. ... Au contraire, se ressouvenant que, parmi le grand nombre des traités de ce philosophe rapportés par Diogène Laërce, il s'en trouve un sous le titre de *Proverbes*, c'est-à-dire de pièces détachées, comme des réflexions ou des remarques, que le premier et le plus grand livre de morale qui ait été fait porte ce même nom dans les divines Ecritures, on s'est trouvé excité par de si grands modèles à suivre selon ses forces une semblable manière d'écrire des moeurs. (14)

The expression *pièces détachées*, adopted by La Bruyère's detractors, later took on a negative connotation; in the eighteenth and nineteenth centuries even supporters like Suard felt obliged to defend him against the accusation of writing in this form. For La Bruyère, however, the phrase has a positive presence which even Barthes, in stating that the *Caractères* are a *livre de fragments*, does not quite catch; for fragment is a broken part of something that was once whole. *Pièce détachée*, on the other hand, has a quite different sense: it might be compared to

[12] The word "charakter" actually comes from a verb which means to scratch or engrave. There is then a shift from engraver to the thing engraved: the stamped impression on a coin, or a mark on the forehead of slaves to identify to whom they belong. Therefore, "character" in the Greek of Theophrastus' time meant an external mark or sign which allowed something to be identified as belonging to a definite class, implying a shift in emphasis from deduction to observational classification.

the expression *pièce d'éloquence* which La Bruyère uses in the *Préface au Discours à l'Académie* (500); a self-contained textual unit. La Bruyère's comments on letters, and what some would now call "l'écriture féminine," also throw light on his attitude toward stylistic continuity in general:

> Ce sexe va plus loin que le nôtre dans ce genre d'écrire ... elles ont un enchaînement de discours inimitable, qui se suit naturellement, *et qui n'est lié que par le sens*. (*Des Ouvrages de l'esprit* 79-80)

La Bruyère praises discontinuous texts like letters, where transitions are determined by shifts in subject matter rather than by a preestablished logical structure or outline. This form of writing clearly attracts him: he is "*excité* par une semblable manière d'écrire."

La Bruyère then goes on to distinguish his work from "deux ouvrages de morale qui sont dans les mains de tout le monde" (15): Pascal's *Pensées* and the *Maximes* of La Rochefoucauld. In his own composition:

> L'on ne suit aucune de ces routes ... il est tout différent des deux autres que je viens de toucher: moins sublime que le premier et moins délicat que le second, il ne tend qu'à rendre l'homme raisonnable, mais par des voies simples et communes, et en l'examinant indifféremment, sans beaucoup de méthode, et selon que les divers chapitres y conduisent, par les âges, les sexes et les conditions, et par les vices, les faibles et le ridicule qui y sont attachés. (15)

The phrase, "l'on ne suit ... par les âges les sexes et les conditions" reflects, as Goyet points out, a *lieu commun* from Aristotle's rhetoric, which in II.12 describes the "nature of characters of men according to their emotions, habits, ages, and fortunes..." (Goyet 5). But the sentences contain typical La Bruyèrian interpolations: *indifféremment, sans beaucoup de méthode*. These may reveal an element of tentativeness on La Bruyère's part, but it is simpler to take what he says at face value: the order of his chapters does not interest him very much. His half-playful admission of the lack of overall composition of his work can be read as a kind of inverse boast, as if to say he is above such considerations.

I will now take up the first version of the Preface to the *Caractères* (1688). In the first sentence, which remains the first sentence throughout all editions, La Bruyère says the *Caractères* are the image of society (that is, of the reader). In the last three sentences, which remain the last three sentences of the Preface in all editions, La Bruyère again distances himself from La Rochefoucauld, as he did in the *Discours sur Théophraste*, by making a distinction between *maximes* and *remarques*:

> Ce ne sont point au reste des maximes que j'aie voulu écrire: elles sont comme des lois dans la morale, et j'avoue que je n'ai ni assez d'autorité ni assez de génie pour faire le législateur; je sais même que j'aurais péché contre l'usage des maximes, qui veut qu'à la manière des oracles elles soient courtes et concises. Quelques-unes de ces remarques le sont, quelques autres sont plus étendues: on pense les choses d'une manière différente, par une sentence, par un raisonnement, par une métaphore ou quelque autre figure ... de là procède la longueur ou la brièveté de mes réflexions. Ceux enfin qui font des maximes veulent être crus: je consens, au contraire, que l'on dise de moi que je n'ai pas quelquefois bien remarqué, pourvu que l'on remarque mieux.

According to La Bruyère, the *maxime* is a more rigid genre, in both form and content, than the *remarque*. Whereas *maximes* should be short and concise, *remarques* can supplely mould themselves to the author's thought. And while *maximes* dictate morality (*elles sont comme des lois dans la morale*), *remarques* merely observe contemporary conduct. The last sentence plays on the two senses of *remarquer* — to see and to say — which also become absorbed by the noun *remarque*. La Bruyère does not claim to *bien remarquer* — to observe society well and write well in some ideal sense. He will have achieved his goal if he observes better, or at least no worse, than anyone else.

Returning to the models of order outlined above (pp. 132-34) to which does La Bruyère's writing show the most affinity? We may infer an answer to this question from the passage above. In his last sentence, La Bruyère distinguishes two kinds of knowledge. Maxims, at least in theory, propose an absolute certainty: "ceux enfin qui font des maximes veulent être crus." *Remarques*, on the other hand, offer a relative sort of truth: "je consens que l'on dise de moi que je n'ai pas quelquefois *bien* remarqué, pourvu que l'on remarque *mieux*." *Remarques* are limited, empirical statements, *maximes*, definitive pronouncements. Going back to Ernst Cassirer's remarks on Pierre Bayle, Cassirer cites Bayle's *Projet d'un dictionnaire critique* (1692): "Historical knowledge belongs to another kind of certainty (*genre de certitude*) than mathematical knowledge... metaphysically it is more certain that an individual named Cicero existed than that any object as defined by pure mathematics really exists." One can see here a kind of analogy with La Bruyère's much less philosophical distinction between *maximes* and *remarques*: La Bruyère separates moral principle or law from social description somewhat in the same way Bayle separates mathematical from historical certainty, thereby creating a space for his own work. Cassirer comments on Bayle's statement: "Such considerations as these give access to the world of fact, but no principle has as yet been developed for taking real possession of this world and for controlling it intellectually. For historical knowledge still represents a mere aggregate, an accumulation of unrelated details exhibiting no inner order. History lies before Bayle like an enormous heap of ruins, and there is no possibility of mastering this abundance of material. To keep up with the rising tide of specialized knowledge would require the inexhaustible assimilative powers of Bayle himself" (203-04) — or La Bruyère.

I would stop short of calling the *Caractères* a *Dictonnaire moral*, but with few changes Cassirer's comments — and especially his metaphors — could be applied to La Bruyère. La Bruyère's concept of sociomoral knowledge informs the order of his work. The organization of the *Caractères* into loosely related, discontinuous *remarques* reflects an intellectual and historical shift from the abstract to the *vécu* (which is very different from the personal or idiosyncratic, terms often applied to his writing). The *Caractères* are an aggregate of *observations morales* which, like Bayle's *Dictionary*, grew by a process of juxtaposition and accretion without aspiring to a logical structure.

Finally, the order of the *Caractères* — and the way that order has been perceived — are reflected in the history of its publication. During La Bruyère's lifetime, the text was printed in paragraph form, with each observation introduced by the typographic sign known as a *pied de mouche*.

During the eighteenth century, the *pieds de mouche* were replaced by asterisks, which reduced the visual and moral distinctness of the individual remarks. But this reduction was minimal compared to the innovations in format — *morceaux choisis*, run-on editions, numbering — which have occurred since. It is almost as though the concept of classification which reached its culmination in the *Encyclopédie* gave way, at the end of the eighteenth century, to new priorities: chronological coherence took precedence over comprehensiveness. La Bruyère's original text did not lack order, but that order, with its implied concepts of distinction and classification, no longer made sense to later readers. It is as if the seventeenth-century text, unintelligible to our eyes, must be reprinted into readability.

Whether we are aware of them or not, these changes in format have affected our reading of La Bruyère. For the reader exposed to the *Caractères* only in excerpts, *morceaux choisis* themselves become a textual form which renders other structures irrelevant. On the other hand, readers of numbered editions assimilate the numbers into their interpretation. A numbered text raises expectations of linear progression; when these expectations are not met by the words themselves, a critical "problem" is created.

However, it would be misleading to suggest that modern difficulties in "following" La Bruyère arise only from the physical alteration of his text. Rather, the dismemberment and reordering of texts like the *Caractères* suggest a underlying change in the concept of knowledge. In the phrase cited earlier, Serge Doubrovsky asserts that La Bruyère's *Caractères* represent "le tragique moderne de l'écriture" (198). Attractive though this formula may be, it is anachronistic. In their own time, polemics aside, the *Caractères* posed no grave problem of reading, let alone a tragedy of writing: tragically obscure texts do not enjoy immediate and multiple reprintings. I would not suggest that we now return to the original format of La Bruyère's work, but our examination of the texts themselves can help to clarify the author's original structural concept. Rather than an array of fragments, the *Caractères* are a collection of *remarques* which constitute a moral reflection of, and on, the world.

6. Conclusion

> Le 'mécanisme' qui a joué ici peut faire l'objet d'une explication savante dont je suis incapable. Cette explication serait valable, voire certaine, mais elle n'en serait pas moins un mystère.
>
> Letter from René Magritte to Michel Foucault, June 4, 1966

This study of four authors has initiated us into four varieties of linguistic experience. For Corneille, the function of language, as rhetoric, is perlocutionary; that is, its success depends on its effect upon the spectator. For example, the *stances du Cid* make Rodrigue an object of sympathy so that, through his suffering, his future actions will be justified to himself and his audience. In this context, both truth and morality become relative issues. It matters little what kind of "truth," if any, is contained inside the character; what counts is the kind of show he puts on. And the individual is an amoral source of energy; as Corneille says of Medea, one may abhor her criminality, but "on admire la source dont elle part." Such characters are creatures of "sang chaud" and intransigence, whose antisocial behavior is tolerated because self-advancement is a legitimate, indeed primary, goal of the individual. And language is an arm of the self in attaining that goal.

This relation between language and the self held audiences' favor in the first part of the seventeenth century: *homo baroco* set well with *homo rhetoricus*. But by mid-century, the view of individual roles as purely performative could no longer be considered adequate. The classical preoccupation with *analyse* — with what goes on in people's heads — and the new awareness of the relation (or the conflict) between what is thought and what is said, gave a greater complexity to discourse and led rhetoric to be called into question. This undermining of rhetoric is evidenced in Racine's early works. What was rhetorical self-assertion for Corneille becomes prevarication in Racine. It is as though the Racinian characters are on a short verbal tether; while they attempt to lie to themselves and to others, they cannot sustain the lies long or easily because the truth underlying their relationships, their feelings, their nature, eventually surfaces. Thus, Hermione attempts to delude herself about her own and Pyrrhus' feelings, but she is inexorably drawn back to reality by the emotional evidence presented: evidence in the French sense of *évidence*, inner certainty. This limited self-delusion is very different from the modernist deception practiced by Jean Cocteau, whose "Menteur" says, "Je suis ... un mensonge qui dit toujours la vérité" (23). There is no subjective truth in Cocteau's character; the center of the onion is hollow. Racine's language, like Corneille's and unlike Cocteau's, is authenticated by the self; unlike Corneille's, its ultimate touchstone is neither will nor energy but passion. In *Iphigénie* and *Phèdre*, the gap between words and truth becomes broader and more serious; as the characters misinterpret messages addressed to them by the gods or fall victim to human deceit, they risk their fortunes and their very lives. Finally, in Racine's biblical plays, this radical uncertainty is resolved by recourse to a transcendent reality to which individual feelings are subordinated. Thus, Ahasuerus' private passion for Esther serves the divinely purposed destiny of the Jews.

Pascal's linguistic concepts form a hierarchy rising from the human to the divine. At its base is human language, which is essentially rhetorical: it aims to satisfy the desires, the *amour-propre* of the speaker. Consequently, the apologist must use rhetorical techniques, must appeal to *amour-propre*, to touch the reader. Human language is also an array of circumscribed, self-limiting and often contradictory truths: *vérité en-deçà des Pyrénees*, *erreur au-delà*. Thus Pascal, in the *Pensées*, evolves a rhetoric of discontinuity and fragmentation, matching both the fracturing of speech and the fractured perceptions of the speaker. The language of Scripture occupies a middle ground between human and divine discourse, meeting the demands of both rhetoric and truth. In his reading of the Bible, Pascal, like Augustine, places an emphasis on figurative language. He follows the Augustinian rule that all passages which make no sense literally must be taken figuratively, as symbols of grace. At the highest level, human discourse disappears as all ordinary referents are replaced with God: His works, the heavens and the earth, represent a single, unchanging Word. But this pure divine discourse is unintelligible on Earth, and Pascal, like Racine, underlines the pitfalls of interpretation, the incompleteness of human understanding. As Sara Melzer puts it, "Language flutters all around the central truth in the hope of eventually reaching it... No matter how complete or precise a sentence may be, it is condemned to remain always at a distance from truth" (217). The only true route to knowledge is through the heart, as inspired by God.

La Bruyère's relation to language is a complex one. First, like Molière, he envisions language in a social context. Speech is the most important of the means by which people assign or deny each other social status. It is also the means, voluntary or involuntary, of revealing their own *caractère* — their basic social being. Nevertheless, La Bruyère does not reduce language to a set of social counters. Even in its most debased form, speech is still the coin of the realm: it still represents the ethical and spiritual values to which he stubbornly clings as a *moraliste*. La Bruyère's concept of sociomoral language informs his work, conveying both the fragmentation of social reality and its moral deterioration. Even the controversial form of the *Caractères* holds meaning. It is impossible to represent society — *ce siècle* — as a moral and social unity, unchanging and identical to itself; all that can be captured are separate fragments of being, which La Bruyère continuously extends to cover the ground. But their mode of relation is juxtaposition, not union; they cannot be forced into the mold of logical completeness. The arbitrariness of La Bruyère's categories, the continual setting up and breaking of logical series, prevents us from reading the *Caractères* as an ordinary essay, and forces us to attend to their discreteness: even the title is plural. Social life is not a satisfyingly coherent whole, and La Bruyère will not allow us to make any more sense of it than it actually possesses.

Thus, La Bruyère's use of language causes him to violate standard notions of structure. What is less obvious is that the great "classical" playwrights, Corneille and Racine, do the same thing. Though both are Aristotelians in their theoretical writings, their plays do not wholly conform to this model. As we have seen, Aristotle's genre categories do not satisfactorily account for Corneille's practice. His comedy results less from the condition of the characters than from the play between rhetoric and truth; tragedy arises only when this play is no longer possible. And the most prevalent Cornelian genre, which I have called drama, consists of a verbal confrontation which is neither comic nor tragic. Racine's *Iphigénie* also bends common genre distinctions: it is a tragicomedy not because it ends "happily" — a young girl is, after all, killed — but because the characters lack knowledge, and thus escape responsibility for their own actions. *Iphigénie* is also tragicomic from a structural standpoint because the characters' plans and imaginings have little effect on the plot's outcome, which rolls on as determined by the gods. While Corneille and Racine both conceptualize their drama within an Aristotelian framework which is the only theoretical construct available to them, their own practice transcends the boundaries of this construct, just as the English language transcends the bounds of the Latin grammatical terminology once used to describe it. Such gaps and confusions between theory and practice strew the history of linguistics and literature; but the double mystique of classicism and Aristotelianism has long maintained its sway on the critical imagination, preventing us from seeing the period in any other terms. It is time to realize that Corneille and Racine's practice does not "violate" Aristotelian tenets; it simply evades them by doing something else.

Beyond these comments on individual authors, what can be said about classical discourse in a larger sense? I will approach this question by a detour into the twentieth century. In *l'usage de la parole*, a painting by the Surrealist Magritte, an index finger pierces through the floor on which is written the word *sirène*, replacing the letter *i*. The finger, dotted by a small bell, does not *represent* the *i* but *supplants* it in a different, third, dimension with which the written word is incommensurable. In this way, Magritte parodies the notion that words point to things; like the ascending staircase in the picture, ending in a blank wall, words lead nowhere beyond themselves. Representation, in other words, is cut off from reference. As Foucault points out in *Ceci n'est pas une pipe*, Magritte's work is typical of twentieth-century art in general in denying the mimetic or representative function: in Magritte's painting, "la représentation ... C'est la dalle d'une tombe" (56-57). Images look like things only in order to remind us they are *not* like them. Further, Magritte's work, in refusing resemblance, also denies any hierarchical principle. "La ressemblance a un 'patron': élément originel qui ordonne et hiérarchise à partir de soi toutes les copies de plus en plus affaiblis qu'on peut en prendre. Ressembler suppose une réference première qui prescrit et classe" (61). It is precisely this reference which is missing from Magritte's paintings. "Hierarchy gives way to a series of exclusively lateral relations" (Introduction to English version 10).

Turning the telescope around to look back at the seventeenth century, one can say, in contrast, that classical discourse affirms both reference and hierarchy. If modern art implies an "antilinguistic program" (Introduction 9), classical art joins discourse to painting, or, rather, painting "reposait silencieusement sur un espace discursif" (71-72) because the affirmation of likeness — *ceci est cela* — is a linguistic structure of subject and predicate. Nevertheless, the classical writers we have examined evince some uneasiness about language. Pascal's work is emblematic in this respect. Like Corneille and Racine, he senses the rhetorical limits of speech, its ties to desire and to illusion. Like La Bruyère's, his style portrays the discontinuity and fragmentation of human speech and perception. And like Racine, he reaches for a truth which is enigmatic, unseeable, difficult to reach, a truth that Magritte will efface with an eraser rub. Thus, the seventeenth century both affirms and undermines its own affirmations, creating an atmosphere of uncertainty which the twentieth century will recognize and make its own. How precarious — and how strong — is the classical order: an *auto da fe* waiting to be lit. Yet the conflagration never occurs. To change the metaphor, classical writing, despite its floatings and ambiguities, always gets back to ground. For Corneille, this "ground" is the innate valor of the hero, a valor both historical and genealogical; for Racine, it is at first the truth of character, later that of transcendence; for Pascal, it is revelation, witnessed in Christ's physical presence on earth or figured in holy writ; for La Bruyère, it is the existence of a moral order, however hidden or ignored.

Along with a principle of truth, classical discourse is upheld by a hierarchical order again implicit in Pascal's model. At the base of the hierarchy is social language, a set of counters which, as La Bruyère and Molière have shown, can easily become counterfeit. Next on the hierarchy comes rhetorical language, more solid than social exchange because it is grounded in the self to which Corneille gives an ultimate value. Racine's psychological truth shares with Corneille's its final validity, but not its moral worth. It is only in the series beginning with *Iphigénie* that the truth of character joins a higher moral order, and that occurs only at the moment of death or through the death of another. This moral discourse is in a sense a subclass of Pascal's religious discourse, true and therefore incomprehensible on earth. Classical language is thus an ascending staircase disappearing not into a blank wall like Magritte's, but into the clouds. In this hierarchy, one cannot ignore the effects of genre — the difference between Corneille and Racine's characters and La Bruyère's *caractères*. Theater — the incarnation of characters on stage — gives more weight to the traits of the individual than aphoristic writing tends to do. But in either case, the underlying thrust of seventeenth-century writing is moralistic in that it is critical, not only of society, but of itself.

This observation leads me back to the knotty question raised in the Introduction of the distinctness of literary discourse. Literary language is distinct not by its structure (since it builds on elements present in everyday speech) but by its direction. Literature is *disorienting*: it gives an extra twist to language. Such is the etymological meaning of the word *trope*: a turn of the linguistic screw. This disorienting twist is called "deviation" by Murray Krieger, "making strange" (*ostranenie*) by the Russian formalists. All these labels refer to a similar reading experience. In giving oneself over to a literary text — be it Balzac or La Bruyère — one feels a kind of displacement: the world of things quivers like a stage backdrop, momentarily revealing, in Bossuet's words, "l'image de notre néant." Of course, Bossuet's "néant" is not our own, but we still understand it and feel it, in our own manner.

Finally, the evidence of this book calls into question the notion of one hegemonic classical discourse.[1] Foucault seems to reject this hegemony in his later works, such as the *History of Sexuality*, when he locates power in the interplay between the ruler and the ruled rather than in the power structure alone. Similarly, writing is situated at an intersection formed by the individual choices of the author and the linguistic and literary patrimony of the past. That is why literary language is both freer and more determined than the material conditions of life "producing" it. On the one hand, writing escapes the efforts of regimes to direct it, of critical schools to define it. On the other hand, it falls short of a total artistic autonomy, *à la* Borgerhoff's *Freedom of French Classicism*. For a text evades the control not only of the powers that be, but of its author as well. The act of writing is informed by a whole series of social, linguistic and psychological forces which the writer cannot fully control, no more than present or future readers can create their own readings *ex nihilo*. In this view, what we

[1] See Erica Harth's excellent discussion of this issue in "Classical Discourse: Gender and Objectivity," which suggests that at least until mid-century, "another voice" than the scientific or objective still was to be heard (*Continuum* 1 [1989] 151-74).

call "literature" is a historic-linguistic continuum which grounds itself anew in each era. Rather than an archeological artifact, cut off in its own space/time layer, I prefer to think of the text as a piece of antique furniture which, in the phrase of the Maine auctioneer, "has some age on it" – which carries with it the patina of previous lives. Hence criticism, like furniture restoring, should be both innovative and preservative. As Steven Marcus has said, it entails a *refabrication* of the text by each epoch and reader, and the greatness of certain texts lies both in their power to attract this refabrication, and in their strength to persevere, even as we force ourselves upon them again and again. In that spirit, let us welcome with open arms – and eyes – modern endeavors to link literature and history, sign and thought, with the uncertainties these explorations inevitably create.

Works Cited

Aeschylus. *The Oresteia*. Tr. Robert Fagles. New York: Bantam Books, 1977.

Aristotle. *Aristotle's Ethics for English Readers*. Tr. H. Rackham. Oxford: Blackwell, 1943.

________. *On the Soul*. Cambridge: Harvard University Press, 1957.

________. *Poetics*. Tr. Leon Golden. Englewood Cliffs: Prentice-Hall, 1968.

________. *Rhetorica*. In *Works*. Ed. W. D. Ross. Oxford: Clarendon, 1908-1952.11.

Aubignac, François Hedelin, abbé de. *Pratique du Théâtre*. Ed. Pierre Martino. Paris: Champion, 1927.

Augustine. *De Trinitate*. In *Patrologia latina cursus completus*, 42. Paris: Migne, 1945.

Bacon, Francis. *The Advancement of Learning*. Ed. Arthur Johnston. In *The Advancement of Learning* and *New Atlantis*. Oxford: Clarendon, 1974. 1-212.

Banfield, Ann. *Unspeakable Sentences: Narration and Representation in the Language of Fiction*. Boston: Routledge and Kegan Paul, 1982.

Barfield, Owen. *Poetic Diction: A Study in Meaning*. New York: McGraw, 1964.

Barnett, Richard. "The Non-Ocularity of Racine's vision." *Orbis literarum* 35.2 (1980) 115-31.

Black, Michael. *Poetic Drama as Mirror of the Will*. New York: Harper and Row, 1977.

Boileau, Nicolas. *Bolaeana*. Amsterdam: An VII de la République.

Borgerhoff, E. B. O. *Freedom of French Classicism*. Princeton: Princeton University Press, 1950.

Burke, Kenneth. *Philosophy of Literary Form*. Berkeley: University of California Press, 1941.

Burkert, Walter. *Homo necans*. Tr. Peter Bing. Berkeley: University of California Press, 1983.

Cahné, Pierre-Alain. *Un Autre Descartes: le philosophe et son langage*. Paris: Vrin, 1980.

Caplan, Jay. "Vicarious *jouissances*: On Reading Casanova." *Modern Language Notes* 100.4 (1985) 803-14.

Cassirer, Ernst. *Philosophy of the Enlightenment.* Princeton: Princeton University Press, 1951.

Cocteau, Jean. "Le Menteur." In *Voix du siècle.* Ed. Smith and Savacool. New York: Harcourt, 1960.

Colish, Rosamund. *The Mirror of Language.* New Haven and London: Yale University Press, 1968.

Corneille, Pierre. *Oeuvres.* Ed. Marty Laveaux. 12 vols. Paris: Hachette, 1910.

________. *Oeuvres complètes.* 2 vols. Paris: Seuil, 1963, 1984.

________. *Théâtre complet.* Ed. Maurice Rat. Paris: Garnier, 1961. Vols. I, II.

________. *Writings on the Theatre.* Ed. H. T. Barnwell. Oxford: Blackwell, 1965.

De Ley, Herbert. *The Movement of Thought.* Urbana and Chicago: University of Illinois Press, 1985.

De Man, Paul. *Blindness and Insight.* Minneapolis: University of Minnesota Press, 1983.

De Mourgues, Odette. *Two French Moralists.* Cambridge: Cambridge University Press, 1978.

Descartes, René. *Discours de la méthode.* In *Oeuvres et lettres.* Paris: Gallimard, 1953.

Doubrovsky, Serge. "Lecture de La Bruyère." *Poétique* 2 (1970) 195-201.

Driver, S. R. *An Introduction to the Literature of the Old Testament.* Cleveland and New York: World Publishing, 1956.

Euripide. *Théâtre complet.* Ed. M. Delcourt-Curvers. Paris: Gallimard, 1962.

Ferguson, Margaret. "Saint Augustine's Region of Unlikeness: The Crossing of Exile and Language." *The Georgia Review* 29.4 (1975) 842-64.

Foucault, Michel. *Les Mots et les choses.* Paris: Gallimard, 1966. Tr. *The Order of Things.* New York: Pantheon, 1970.

________. *L'Archéologie du savoir.* Paris: Gallimard, 1969. *The Archaeology of Knowledge.* Tr. A. M. Sheridan Smith. New York: Harper and Row, 1972.

________. *History of Sexuality.* New York: Pantheon, 1978.

________. *Ceci n'est pas une pipe.* Fata Morgana, 1973. *This Is Not a Pipe.* Tr. James Harkness. Berkeley: University of California Press, 1983.

Furetière, Antoine. *Dictionnaire universel.* 3 vols. Paris: SNL-Le Robert, 1978.

Garapon, Robert. *La Fantaisie verbale et le comique dans le théâtre français.* Paris: Colin, 1957.

Geertz, Clifford. *Works and Lives.* Stanford: Stanford University Press, 1988.

Genette, Gérard. "La Rhétorique restreinte." In *Figures III.* Paris: Seuil, 1972.

Giraud, Pierre. *La Sémiologie.* Paris: Presses Universitaires de France, 1971. Tr. George Gross. London and Boston: Routledge and Kegan Paul, 1975.

Goldsmith, Oliver. *Collected Works.* Ed. Arthur Friedman. Oxford: Clarendon, 1966.

Grene, David and Richard Lattimore, eds. *Greek Tragedies* II. Chicago: University of Chicago Press, 1960.

Harth, Erica. "Classical Disproportion: La Bruyère's *Caractères*." *Esprit Créateur* 15.1-2 (Spring-Summer 1975) 189-210.

Homer. *The Iliad*. Tr. Richard Lattimore. Chicago: University of Chicago Press, 1961.

Hoy, David. "Foucault's Slalom." *London Review of Books* 4-17 November 1982: 18.

Johnson, Mark, ed. *Philosophical Perspectives on Metaphor*. Minneapolis: University of Minnesota Press, 1981.

Krieger, Murray. *Theory of Criticism*. Baltimore: Johns Hopkins University Press, 1976.

Kuhn, Thomas. *The Essential Tension*. Chicago: University of Chicago Press, 1977.

La Bruyère, Jean de. *Les Caractères*. Paris: Didot, 1813. Notice by Suard.

________. *Oeuvres*. 3 vols. Ed. Gustave Servois. Paris: Hachette - Les Grand Ecrivains de la France, 1865-1832.

La Capra, Dominick. *Rethinking Intellectual History*. Ithaca and London: Cornell University Press, 1983.

Lanham, Richard. *The Motives of Eloquence*. New Haven: Yale University Press, 1976.

Lasserre, Françoise. "Avant *L'Illusion* ... Clitandre." *PFSCL* 14.27 (1987) 703-32.

________. 'La Reflexion sur le théâtre dans les comédies de Corneille." *PFSCL* 13.24 (1986) 283-312.

Laubriet, P. "A Propos des *Caractères*: ordre ou fantaisie?" *RHLF* 67 (1967) 502-17.

Lefever, André. *Literary Knowledge*. Assen/Amsterdam: Van Gorcum, 1977.

Le Gras, Advocat au Parlement. *La Rethorique françoise*. Paris, 1672.

Littré, Paul-Emile. *Dictionnaire de la langue française*. Edition nouvelle. Chicago: Encyclopedia Britannica, 1982.

Lynn, Steven. "The Epistemological Status of Literary and Scientific Discourse." Unpublished paper, 1983.

Malebranche, Nicolas. *Oeuvres*. Paris: Pléiade, 1979. Vol. I.

Marcus, Steven. *Partisan Review* Conference, Boston University, 14 September 1979.

Marin, Louis. "Puss-in-Boots: Power of Signs — Signs of Power." *Diacritics* 7 (June 1977).

Melzer, Sara. "Pascal's *Pensées*: Economy and the Interpretation of Fragments." *Stanford French Review* 6.2-3 (1982) 207-20.

Miel, Jan. *Pascal and Theology*. Baltimore and London: The Johns Hopkins University Press, 1969.

Muratore, M. J. "Racinian Stasis." In *Relectures raciniennes*. Ed. Richard L. Barnett. Paris: Biblio 17 (1986) 113-25.

________. "Theater as Theater: The Language of Cornelian Illusion." *Romanic Review* 86.1 (1983) 12-23.

Olivet, l'abbé d'. *Histoire de l'Académie Française*. Paris: Livet, 1858.

Ovid. *Metamorphoses*. Tr. Mary M. Innes. New York: Penguin Books, 1955.

Pascal, Blaise. *Oeuvres complètes*. Ed. Lafuma. Paris: Seuil, 1963.

Perelman, Chaim, and Olbrechts-Tyteca, Lucie. *Rhétorique et philosophie*. Paris: Presses Universitaires de France, 1952.

Racevskis, Karlis. *Michel Foucault and the Subversion of Intellect*. Ithaca: Cornell University Press, 1983.

Racine, Jean. *Oeuvres complètes*. 2 vols. Ed. Raymond Picard. Paris: Gallimard, 1950-1966.

Reiss, Timothy. *The Discourse of Modernism*. Ithaca: Cornell University Press, 1982.

________. *Truth and Tragedy*. New Haven: Yale University Press, 1980.

Richards, I. A. *The Philosophy of Rhetoric*. New York: Oxford University Press, 1965.

Riffaterre, Michael. *Semiotics of Poetry*. Bloomington: Indiana University Press, 1978.

Romanowski, Sylvie. *L'Illusion chez Descartes*. Paris: Klincksieck, 1974.

Rorty, Richard. *Philosophy and the Mirror of Nature*. Princeton: Princeton University Press, 1979.

Rotrou, Jean. *Oeuvres*. Paris: Th. Desoer, Libraire, 1820.

Rousset, Jean. *La Littérature de l'âge baroque en France*. Paris: Corti, 1954.

Sandmel, Samuel. *The Hebrew Scriptures*. New York: Knopf, 1963.

Science, Language and the Perspective Mind. Yale French Studies 49 (1973).

Searle, John R. "The Word Turned Upside Down." *The New York Review of Books* 27 October 1983: 74-79.

Shamir, Yehuda. "Mystic Jerusalem." *Studia Mystica* 3.2 (Summer 1980) 50-60.

Spitzer, Leo. "Language: The Basis of Science, Philosophy, and Poetry." In George Boas, ed. *Studies in Intellectual History*. Baltimore: Johns Hopkins University Press, 1935.

________. "Le Récit de Théramène." In *Linguistics and Literary History*. Princeton: Princeton University Press, 1948. 87-134.

Stempel, Daniel. "Blake, Foucault and the Classical Episteme." *PMLA* 96.3 (1981) 388-407.

Taylor, Charles. "Interpretation and the Sciences of Man." *Review of Metaphysics* 25 (1971).

Thurber, James. *The White Deer*. New York: Harcourt, 1945.

Turnell, Martin. *The Classical Moment*. Norfolk: New Directions, n.d.

Van Baelen, Jacqueline. "The Rhetoric of Theatrality in the Later Tragedies of Corneille." *PFSCL* 7 (1977) 63-80.

Van Delft, Louis. *La Bruyère moraliste: quatre études sur les Caractères*. Geneva: Droz, 1971.

Virgile. *Enéides* I-VI. Ed. Henri Goeltzer. Paris: Société d'Editions Les Belles Lettres, 1970.

________. *Aeneid.* Tr. Robert Fitzgerald. New York: Random House, 1981.

Whitehead, Alfred North. *Science and the Modern World.* New York: Pelican Mentor Books, 1948.

Woshinsky, Barbara R. *La Princesse de Clèves: The Tension of Elegance.* The Hague: Mouton, 1973.

________. "Two Concepts of Language in Molière's *Dom Juan.*" *Romanic Review* 72.4 (1981) 401-08.

Zimmermann, Eléonore. *La Liberté et le destin dans le théâtre de Jean Racine.* Stanford French and Italian Studies 24. Saratoga: Anma Libri, 1982.